The History of British Rock 'n' Roll:

The Forgotten Years 1956 - 1962

Also by Robin Bell:

How Swede It Is
©Copyright 2005 by Robin Bell
ISBN: 978-1-4476-2218-5

The Australian Outback – The History and Mythology of the Land Down-Under
©Copyright 2006 by Robin Bell
ISBN: 978-1-4475-5275-8

The Road To The Hermitage
©Copyright 2006 by Robin Bell
ISBN: 978-91-981283-8-3

Books for Children:

My Adventure Series:

Discovering Australia	ISBN: 978-91-981283-0-7
Discovering America	ISBN: 978-91-981283-1-4
With Pirates	ISBN: 978-91-981283-3-8
In Sweden	ISBN: 978-91-981283-6-9
In Space	ISBN: 978-91-981916-0-8
Under the Ocean	ISBN: 978-91-981283-9-0

Advanced My Adventure Series:

In Australia	ISBN: 978-91-981283-2-1
With Pirates	ISBN: 978-91-981283-4-5
With the Loch Ness Monster	ISBN: 978-91-981283-5-2

The History of British Rock 'n' Roll:
The Forgotten Years 1956 - 1962

Robin Bell

Robin Bell Books
Sweden
ISBN: 978-91-981283-7-6

First Printing: 2014

ISBN 978-91-981283-7-6

Robin Bell Books
Ölme Hagen
68194 Kristinehamn
Sweden

www.robinbell.se

Ordering Information:
Special discounts are available on quantity purchases by corporations, associations, educators, and others. For details, contact the publisher at the above listed address.

U.S. trade bookstores and wholesalers: Please contact Robin Bell Books

Email robin@robinbell.se

Dedication

To the millions of listeners to the music
To the tens of thousands of would be rock 'n' rollers
To the thousands who played the music
To the hundreds who made the music

Contents

Illustrations

Acknowledgements

I have dreamed of writing this book for years, but other commitments have kept me away from the research needed. It was not until I heard the song "Class Of '58" by Al Stewart on his CD *A Beach Full Of Shells* that I seriously sat down at my computer and started writing.

It has been a fascinating journey as each topic has led me further into areas from my teenage years that I thought that I had forgotten.

My thanks go to the many recording artists, producers, writers, composers and manufacturers who have made information widely available through the Internet – an unbelievable source of facts and figures, often confusing and contradictory.

Thanks also to Al Stewart for the kick-start I needed to begin this book, for the years of enjoyment from his many records and to Frabjous Music for permission to use the quotations shown under each chapter heading. Visit Al's web site for tour dates, records and much more at http://www.alstewart.com/

Very many thanks to Steve Russell for the photographs of the two guitars on the cover – a Futurama Colorama and a Höfner President – for the photos of amplifiers and other gear and for the many comments, suggestions and corrections, particularly in the area of the history of the Höfner and Framus guitar manufacturing companies.

His web site (http://www.vintagehofner.co.uk/) has a multitude of photos and fascinating information on many of the guitars used by early British rock 'n' roll musicians. I can recommend Steve's book 'Höfner – The Complete Violin Bass Story' for readers who want the full details of these remarkable manufacturers.

Thanks to Barrie Smith for his excellent photos of Lonnie Donegan, Tommy Steele and The Steelmen and Russ Hamilton. Barrie has a web site (http://www.frenchpix.com/rock.n.roll.html) with more great photos which is well worth a visit.

My thanks go to Alice Moschetti, Licensing Executive at the Victoria and Albert Museum, London (visit the web site at http://www.vandaimages.com/) for her invaluable assistance with photos from the Harry Hammond collection used in this book.

Special thanks to Gordon Thompson, Department of Music, Skidmore College, Saratoga Springs, New York for his excellent web site *1960s British Rock and Pop*, (http://www.skidmore.edu/~gthompso/britrock/60brchro/index.html) which served as a valuable starting point for further research. Another extremely useful web site is at *Classic UK 45s* (http://www.45-rpm.org.uk/) which has a great wealth of detail on recordings and artists biographies.

Preface

If you ask someone about the story of popular music in Britain during the 1950's and 1960's, the chances are that they will mention Bill Haley, Rock 'n' Roll and then The Beatles.

But seldom will they talk about that short period of time in between, when Britain developed its own style of rock 'n' roll; when artists such as Tommy Steele, Marty Wilde and Cliff Richard became household names and when the recording industry in Britain underwent radical changes.

As a youngster growing up in England in the 1950's and 1960's, I first became aware of rock 'n' roll music through 78 rpm records played on our old wind-up gramophone using steel or thorn needles and through the crackling, fading radio reception of Radio Luxembourg.

One of our first records was a 78 rpm shellac version of Elvis Presley's "All Shook Up". Our copy suffered an unfortunate knee on it, which caused a crack to spread from the centre to the outside. I'm not sure how, but the click caused by needle hitting that crack seemed to be in perfect synchronization with the beat. Of course, the flip side "That's When Your Heartaches Begin" was rarely played – that wasn't rock 'n' roll and besides, the click was off beat on that side.

My first 45 rpm vinyl record was Marty Wilde's "Endless Sleep" which unfortunately I tried to play on that old wind-up gramophone. I watched fascinated as a small spiral of plastic emerged from the steel needle as it landed on the vinyl record before I realised my mistake and saved Marty from his own endless sleep.

Luckily, we soon graduated to a 'real' record player – one that didn't need the needle to be re-sharpened every couple of plays and didn't require rewinding either – and which was safe for those precious vinyl 45's.

Now we didn't have to strain through the static in the evenings to our heroes coming from Radio Luxembourg, 208 on your dial. No more interruptions while we heard the virtues of Charles Atlas extolled, or discovered the magical and mysterious pools winning system of Horace Batchelor, when all we wanted was to hear the beat from the rapidly growing up baby of rhythm and blues that was rock 'n' roll.

Eventually we had our own local heroes as first skiffle – that peculiarly British combination of country, folk and traditional jazz – swept across the country. Then, boosted by the simplicity of the music, teenagers developed their own version of the American phenomenon that was rock 'n' roll and British rock 'n' roll artists started to appear in the UK charts.

Like many others of the time, I longed for a guitar and eventually persuaded my mother to buy me one – from memory it cost us around 17 shillings and sixpence. The action was unbelievably high, making it almost impossible to play, but I persevered and worked my way through the classic Bert Weedon book *Play In A Day* – which I still have.

Although unplayable, I was still able to 'play' that guitar in front of the mirror at home as I listened to Tommy Steele and Cliff Richard on the record player.

Later on I tried making my own guitars – the first a single cutaway acoustic painstakingly made from plywood, steamed and bent around wooden formers and then spray painted sky blue with automobile cellulose paint by a friend serving an apprenticeship at the local garage – thanks Michael.

My first solid was cut from a single plank of wood, with help from my grandfather, and this time I got the colour right when I hand painted it bright red. With frets and strings rescued from a discarded acoustic guitar, a microphone screwed under the strings as a pick-up, it sounded awful connected to our mains radio as a make-do amplifier.

While still at school I was able to go to watch some of those Larry Parnes package tours as they visited the Gaumont Theatre at Ipswich or the Windmill Theatre at Great Yarmouth – Tommy Steele, Joe Brown and The Bruvvers, Billy Fury and The Tornados, Peter Jay and The Jaywalkers, Helen Shapiro and visiting American super heroes such as Little Richard, Bo Diddley, Charlie and Inez Fox, Roy Orbison and The Everly Brothers.

I managed to catch up with The Beatles and The Rolling Stones on their first British tours – but even in those early years the screams from the audience drowned out the music.

Even in our sleepy part of the country, skiffle and rock 'n' roll were king and soon there were local groups to play live at our Village Fetes and youth clubs. Groups such as Roger and The Rockets, The Wenhaston Strollers and our local favourites, formed from school friends, The Rebels, who later went on to find fame – if not fortune – as The Wild Oats, and managed to gain a recording contract.

The Wild Oats limited edition EP, containing "You Can't Judge A Book By Its Cover", Walking The Dog", Will You Still Love Me Tomorrow" and "Put The Blame On Me" recorded in 1963 on the Oak record label at the R.G. Jones recording studio in Morden, Surrey – where artists such as The Rolling Stones, The Kinks and The Yardbirds had all cut demonstration records – gained cult status locally but failed to gain national exposure.

Later on I moved away from home to London. It was an amazing experience to be a teenager in London during the 'Swinging Sixties' and despite the saying, I was there and yes, I can remember most of it.

Memories abound, such as John Mayall's Bluesbreakers at Earls Court, or Pink Floyd, complete with light show, in the open air at Goldsmith's College. Or how about Geno Washington and The Ram-Jam Band – or The Bonzo Dog Doo-Dah Band at the Fairfield Halls, Croydon.

But those will have to wait for the second volume of the series. This book concentrates on those early, almost forgotten years when every kid wanted to be Elvis and for a brief period it all seemed so possible before the music calmed down again.

Of course it couldn't last. The establishment fought back against this unbridled enthusiastic music and sanitized it. The rawness of rock 'n' roll was gradually replaced by the middle-of-the-road blandness of squeaky clean balladeers.

The music that had excited, tantalized, offended and raised the hopes of so many now sank slowly in a sea of mediocrity. But somewhere a spark still glowed faintly, a spark which would be fanned and turned into an inferno that would consume the world.

This then is the story of the forgotten years, when a musical revolution played out in Britain and paved the way for the conflagration to come.

Introduction

"Rock 'n' Roll's not good or bad, it's just the sound of being young"

So sang Al Stewart in his "Class of '58"[1] song written as a stark reminder of the highs and lows of the early British rock 'n' rollers.

For a few brief years at the end of the 1950's, British rock 'n' roll burned brightly across a country that was beginning to free itself from the shackles of war time austerity.

In the middle of the 1950's rock 'n' roll found its way to the British Isles and was greedily accepted by the teenagers there. Artists such as Tommy Steele, Marty Wilde and Cliff Richard provided the British youth with a chance to see live, on stage, the exciting phenomenon that they had only experienced before on film, through Radio Luxembourg or imported records

But that flame was quickly dampened, leaving behind a blandness in the music that was all too familiar as the "Brylcreem Boys" took over. But the flame was not extinguished – a glowing ember remained that was soon to burst into a conflagration that would lead to the greatest social upheaval the world had seen.

In the mid 1960's the world capitulated to the assault of British popular music. Musical charts across the globe were dominated by artists and groups originating in England, Scotland, Wales and Ireland. Teenagers across the globe responded to the forces of change that started in England – forces that were set in motion by those first few British musical pioneers.

While just a decade before the dominating musical force was based in the United States of America, the balance suddenly swung to the British Isles with a suddenness that astounded the world.

But to understand why and how this happened, we need to look more deeply at the social and economic conditions that existed in Britain in the 1950's and 1960's.

The end of the Second World War, with all the excitement and anticipation it created, did nothing to improve the living conditions of the British population. Of course the constant fear of bombs was over, but the physical and economic damage had been done.

Britain was short of everything – housing, food, clothing, even cash. With so much destruction in the bomb-ravaged cities, housing was a prime priority and many families – including my own – were living in temporary accommodation, known affectionately as "pre-fabs."[2] This temporary accommodation remained our home until 1968. Ration books were issued and it seemed as if the road to recovery for the country would indeed be a long and winding one.

Before the full scale assault of television and with many cinemas and dance halls bombed out, entertainment was largely confined to radio, with the airwaves dominated by the British Broadcasting Corporation (the BBC, or "Beeb" as it was affectionately known.)

The Beeb had a monopoly on radio broadcasts in Britain and supplied a mix of radio programmes through the imaginatively named Light Programme, the Home Service and the Third Programme. While the Home Service and the Third Programme offered classical music, drama and educational services, the Light Programme took its name from the mixture of light entertainment, musical offerings, comedy shows and radio serials.

Throughout the 1950's and early 1960's, the Light Programme schedules were still geared to the years of the war. "Workers Playtime", designed to enliven the mundane jobs of the unfortunates in the factories, was a typical example. First broadcast in 1941, the programme was broadcast three times weekly from factory canteens across the land until 1964 and highlighted the vocal and comedy artists of the era, such as Eve Boswell, Dorothy Squires, Anne Shelton, Peter Sellers and Morecambe and Wise.

Sunday lunchtimes were not complete without "The Billy Cotton Band Show", hosted by the cockney band leader and regular artists such as Alan Breeze and Kathy Kay. The jokes for the show were often scripted by Terry Jones and Michael Palin, later to gain fame as members of *Monty Python's Flying Circus*.

But across the Atlantic, the United States enjoyed a much richer economy. Teenagers were more affluent than their European counterparts and although the threats of the war years had been replaced by a strong sense of conservatism and a belief in the American way of life – at least among the adult population – the American youth had the money to spend on entertainment and self-expression.

After the war, American music was dominated by the white, pop market with artists such as Bing Crosby, Doris Day and Frank Sinatra. With a repertoire dominated by ballads and love songs, the smooth, polished, clean-cut music had little in common with the growing desire of the younger generation to embrace a rawer, basic form of music.

The spirit of rebellion from the attitude of their parents' generation was fuelled by the rise of rock 'n' roll music in the 1950's. The driving beat of this "new" music and the explicit lyrics perfectly expressed the mood of the young generation – it was suitably offensive to their parents and reflected the growing gap between the youth and the "oldies."

By 1952 early rhythm and blues music as performed by Fats Domino, Howlin' Wolf and Muddy Waters had been discovered by the American youth and radio disc jockeys such as Alan Freed in Cleveland and later New York City began playing this exciting new music to a rapidly growing audience of teenagers.

As records by predominantly black artists began to appear in the pop charts, the larger record labels began to produce cover versions of these hits. But white artists, too, began to appreciate the power and popularity of the original artists and in 1954, Bill Haley, who had served his apprenticeship with a series of country-based bands, began to incorporate more of the rhythm and blues style and energy into his own music.

The result was the classic "Rock Around The Clock" and the even more successful "Shake, Rattle And Roll", which featured in the Billboard charts for over six months and resulted in Bill Haley's first gold record. Rock 'n' Roll had arrived – at least in the United States.

Even though the BBC had a monopoly on radio broadcasts within Britain, the teenagers had an alternative source of music – at least in the evenings. Radio Luxembourg, started in 1933, fought a constant battle with the BBC, who considered it "a scandal, insolent and a pirate."

Radio Luxembourg had been allocated a low-power frequency on the medium wave band and was intended to provide services to Luxembourg – a country with a land area no larger than that of Greater London. The station refused to accept the frequency offered and instead elected to broadcast on the long waveband, claiming that it needed the greater coverage afforded by the long wave to support operations involving foreign language commercials.

The BBC continued to oppose Radio Luxembourg up to the start of World War 2, but softened their attitude towards previous "disc jockeys" that were forced to leave the station when Germany took over operations during the war. Several of the Radio Luxembourg presenters even found jobs at the BBC, but the sound of Radio Luxembourg changed totally during the war years as William Joyce – less than affectionately known by British listeners as Lord Haw-Haw – broadcast Nazi propaganda aimed at Britain.

American psychological army forces took over Radio Luxembourg towards the end of the war in 1945, with Britain's backing, with broadcasts firstly aimed at boosting morale of prisoners of war in Europe. At the end of the war, the Americans turned it back to an entertainment station for a short while, but in 1946 Radio Luxembourg was back on air broadcasting sponsored English programmes.

In 1948 Radio Luxembourg broadcast the first top 20 music chart to British listeners and the station continued to grow throughout the late 1940's and the beginning of the1950's, adding quiz shows, radio plays and comedy shows to the mix.

However, once again the BBC was alarmed at the threat posed by the interloper from the continent. While many listeners were convinced that Radio Luxembourg was actually broadcasting from within Britain, the French owners decided in 1951 to use the long wave transmissions for the expanding French services and the English transmissions were switched back to the medium wave again, to the magical frequency of 208 meters.

The switch back to the medium wave, despite the difficulties in reception and broadcasting hours restricted to evenings only did little to dampen the enthusiasm of teenagers in Britain who were keen to hear more of the exciting new American sounds beamed in to eager ears. Radio 208 was the introduction to rock 'n' roll for many a weary teenager – and their worried parents.

By 1956, social conditions in Britain had changed for the better from the constantly grey, drab and dowdy way of life existing just after the war. The economy was recovering; unemployment was falling as American multinational corporations began to establish themselves in Britain for an onslaught in to Europe. In 1957 the Prime Minister, Harold Macmillan, had gone so far as to state complacently "You've never had it so good."[3]

Macmillan's comment would not apply to the youth of the time in a country living in what has been described as "an old man's country." All over the country the seeds of the coming revolution were being sown. Teenagers now had more money, the universities were showing signs of radicalism and the youth were listening more and more to the reports of the youth culture emanating from America.

But whereas the American youth culture had been controlled to some extent by the authorities, in Britain it was embraced by the youth and grew into the phenomenon that became known for all time as the Swinging Sixties. The teenagers in the United Kingdom in the mid 1950's and early 1960's had survived the war, they were determined to take control of their own destinies, they had their own money and they wanted the world – now.

Chapter One: In the Beginning...

"Doing bad cover versions of American hits"
(Al Stewart – Class of '58)

A look through the UK charts of 1954 and 1955 is a depressing sight for aficionados of rock 'n' roll. The top five records of 1954 were, in order, Doris Day with "Secret Love", David Whitfield and Mantovani's Orchestra with "Cara Mia", the trumpeter Eddie Calvert with "Oh Mein Papa", Kitty Kallen with "Little Things Mean a Lot" and finally the Obernkirchen Children's Choir with "The Happy Wanderer".

You need to look a long way down until you come to Bill Haley and his Comets with "Shake, Rattle and Roll" down in 75th place in the top 100 for 1954 – and that as a direct result of the record reaching a high of number 4 in the UK charts in December, 1954.

1955 doesn't provide a great deal of comfort either, at least for British rock 'n' roll artists. The top five charting records in the UK for that year show a similar mix as the previous year, with artists such as Tennessee Ernie Ford ("Give Me Your Word"), Slim Whitman ("Rose Marie") and Frankie Laine ("Cool Water") featuring at the top.

Again, the honour for the highest placing rock 'n' roll record of the year went to Bill Haley and His Comets with "Rock Around The Clock" listed at number 15 for the year, thanks to its number 1 placing in October and November, 1955.

In the main, though, the charts were filled with the easy listening American vocalists such as Johnny Ray, Tony Bennett, Pat Boone and Frank Sinatra and their British equivalents David Whitfield, Dickie Valentine and Ronnie Hilton.

The war years had boosted the popularity of patriotic singers such as Bing Crosby and The Andrews Sisters, and in the years following the end of the war, Americans adults wanted their entertainers to be true representations of the American way of life – true to the cause, clean cut and definitely not rebellious.

But under the surface, American youth was tiring of this smoothness and clinically clean approach – they wanted more excitement and found it among the radio airwaves, especially among the black orientated gospel radio stations and those playing rhythm and blues music.

While white teenagers in America could be found listening to the radio stations aimed at black audiences, playing what was called at the time 'race music', the opposite was also true, as young black teenagers often tuned in to the stations broadcasting country music.

It was this cross-over and blending between gospel, rhythm and blues and country music which helped give birth to rock 'n' roll, although the term had been used as early as the 1930's, first by the Boswell Sisters in the 1934 movie *Transatlantic Merry-Go-Round* as they sang "Rock and Roll" and later by the country singer Buddy Jones on his 1939 Decca recording of "Rockin', Rollin' Mama".

In the early 1950's, the rumblings of rock 'n' roll could be heard getting louder and louder. Sam Phillips in Memphis, Tennessee had already produced what was arguably the first ever real rock 'n' roll record, "Rocket 88"[4] – a tribute to the fastest road car in America at the time, the Oldsmobile 88 – credited to Jackie Brenston and his Delta Cats (in reality Ike Turner's Kings of Rhythm) in 1951.

The revenues from that record helped Phillips found his legendary company Sun Records, from which would emerge some of the greatest early rock 'n' roll recordings.

Initially Sam Phillips founded Sun as a means to be able to record the many black artists in the South who were unable to put their music on record. A similar reasoning could be found in Chicago, where

Leonard Chess saw that the city had become a centre for black musicians from the Deep South where he founded Chess Records.

In 1952 Willie Mae 'Big Mama' Thornton was heard singing by the singer and band leader Johnny Otis, as she cleaned a room at the hotel in which Otis was staying in Houston, Texas.

Otis brought her to Los Angeles where she recorded the Lieber-Stoller classic "Hound Dog" in the famous Radio Recorders Studio on August 13, 1952. The record was not released until February, 1953 on the Peacock label and by late March that year had reached the Billboard Rhythm and Blues charts.

The success of the record helped the cross-over of rhythm and blues music into rock 'n' roll with its backing music limited to just guitar, bass and drums, leaving out the traditional saxophones and piano which had previously been the hall mark of rhythm and blues records.

From the other side of the equation, country music was honing its contribution to rock 'n' roll, in the perhaps unlikely shape of the former Indiana State Yodelling Champion William John Clifton Haley – better known as Bill.

Bill Haley learned his chops in the 1940's when he sang with a number of bands such as The Down Homers in Connecticut, before forming his own group, which he named Bill Haley's Saddlemen.

In 1952 the group changed name to become Bill Haley with Haley's Comets and as such recorded their first ever Billboard chart success "Crazy Man, Crazy", described as the first white rock 'n' roll hit.

Shortly after, the group changed name again to Bill Haley and His Comets and in 1954 recorded the now legendary "Rock Around The Clock". The song was a slow starter, staying in the US charts for just a week before fading. Bill Haley and His Comets had in the meantime recorded a cover version of "Shake, Rattle and Roll" – originally recorded by Big Joe Turner the same year.

"Shake, Rattle and Roll" – with the somewhat suggestive lyrics cleaned up and given a more countrified 'Western Swing' arrangement by Bill Haley – became the first rock 'n' roll record to enter the UK charts in December, 1954.

But in Britain up until that time the same ethics applied as in America, and the British charts were filled with light, non-threatening, some might say superficial or trivial songs far removed from the realities of post war Britain. Entertainers who had enjoyed success during the war continued to provide the majority of popular music during the early 1950's.

Records by the popular Billy Cotton Orchestra – who had his regular Sunday lunchtime programme on the BBC radio running from 1949 right up to 1968 – and the singer/comedian Norman Wisdom ("Don't Laugh at Me, ('Cause I'm a Fool)") jostled for chart positions with the likes of Max Bygraves ("Gilly Gilly Ossenfeffer Katzenellen Bogen by the Sea") and Joe (Mr. Piano) Henderson ("Sing it With Joe").

Singers such as Dickie Valentine and Dennis Lotis were typical of the male British singers of the 1950's – basically light operatic voices who performed in front of the popular big bands of the time, such as The Ted Heath Orchestra.

A dispute between the American Federation of Musicians (AFM) and the British Musicians Union (MU) had caused problems in both countries, with restrictions in place on American acts being allowed to perform in Britain and vice versa.

This dispute began to ease in 1955 when an agreement was reached between the AFM and the MU allowing some American performers being allowed to perform in Britain, providing a similar number of British performers could perform in America.

One of the first to benefit from this easing was The Ted Heath Orchestra, which was allowed to tour in America while The Stan Kenton Orchestra reciprocated with a British tour.

The Ted Heath Orchestra undoubtedly gained valuable insight into the music scene in America during this visit and was able to exploit this experience in Britain with the addition of the singers Dickie Valentine, Lita Rosa and Dennis Lotis, designed to add more appeal to a younger audience.

But there was another twist to the tale in England. While American jazz musicians tended to favour swing style jazz, in England the preference was for Dixieland jazz – more commonly known as traditional or Trad Jazz.

So at the same time that Elvis Presley was recording in Sun Studios in Memphis, under the legendary Sam Phillips, together with the likes of Carl Perkins, Jerry Lee Lewis and Johnny Cash, in Britain Trad Jazz was increasingly becoming more popular.

Among the proponents of this style of music was The Chris Barber Jazz Band, featuring the banjo player, Anthony James – better known as "Lonnie" – Donegan.

On July 13th, 1955 during a coffee break in a recording session for the jazz band, the band leader, Chris Barber, and Lonnie Donegan persuaded the recording engineer to let them try a "couple of our skiffle numbers," which were proving successful during live dates. The style of the songs was based on traditional American folk music, but with a jazz content, and was christened skiffle, after the American group Dan Burley and His Skiffle Boys[5].

The results of that impromptu recording session were the songs "Rock Island Line" – composed by the American folk and blues musician Huddie Ledbetter, better known simply as Lead Belly – and "John Henry", a song about an American folk hero.

In January, 1956, "Rock Island Line" was a hit in both Britain and America, sold a million copies worldwide and the skiffle craze had hit Britain with a vengeance. More Lonnie Donegan skiffle hits followed during the year, such as "Lost John" and "Bring a Little Water, Sylvie" and his success continued in 1957, with records such as "Putting on the Style", "Cumberland Gap" and "Don't You Rock Me, Daddy-O".

Figure 1 - Lonnie Donegan
Lonnie Donegan, the king of skiffle music on the set of The 6-5 Special.
Photo courtesy Barrie Smith

The success of skiffle was partly based on the lack of the necessity for expensive musical instruments or high levels of musicianship. Teenagers across Britain could and did make or purchase their own cheap instruments – guitars, stand-up broomstick basses and washboards – to emulate the sounds of Lonnie Donegan and other successful skiffle artists such as Chas McDevitt and The Vipers

But while skiffle gave British youngsters a chance to break free from the strict musical tastes of their parents, it was the inclusion of "Rock Around The Clock" in the 1955 movie *'Blackboard Jungle'* that kick started the rock 'n' roll phenomenon in Britain and prompted the skiffle playing youth of Britain to look further afield for their inspiration.

With Radio Luxembourg supplying the hungry teenagers of Britain with the sounds and news of the latest records and singing sensations from America, and port cities such as London and Liverpool introducing American records by sailors who brought copies in to the country from overseas voyages, the rock 'n' roll freight train became an unstoppable force.

1956 was the year that rock 'n' roll really arrived in Britain. Bill Haley and His Comets had no less than seven chart successes during the year with "Rock Around the Clock" still charting in January, followed by – in no particular order – "Rockin' Through the Rye", "The Saints Rock 'n' Roll", "See You Later, Alligator", "Rip It Up", "Rock-A-Beatin' Boogie" and "Razzle Dazzle".

Buoyed by the success of Haley and His Comets, the English jazz drummer and bandleader Tony Crombie formed a rock 'n' roll group called The Rockets in 1956, loosely based on the Bill Haley arrangements and featuring – for a short time at least – one Jet Harris, later to gain fame in The Shadows, on bass guitar.

The new group's first record, "(We're Goin' to) Teach You To Rock" was a cover version of the version by the American group Freddie Bell and The Bellboys – who had also coincidentally just released their version of "Hound Dog". The Tony Crombie and The Rockets version of "Teach You to Rock", produced by Norrie Paramor, reached number 25 in the UK charts in October, 1956 and is credited as the first British rock 'n' roll record.

Other notable musicians to later feature in The Rockets were Ronnie Scott and Tubby Hayes, although by this time the group were mainly a jazz group.

Figure 2 - Tony Crombie and The Rockets
Tony Crombie's cover version of the Freddie Bell and The Bellboys 'We're Gonna Teach You To Rock' is considered the first British Rock 'n' Roll record.
© Victoria and Albert Museum, London.

Apart from this British success, and the skiffle boys – and girls – the American recordings continued to fill the UK charts. Among the rock 'n' roll records to hit the UK charts during 1956 were releases by Carl Perkins ("Blue Suede Shoes"), Frankie Lymon and The Teenagers ("Why Do Fools Fall In Love" and Gene Vincent ("Be Bop A Lula").

One British singer to take advantage of the American songs, by recording cover versions, was the variety singer popular in the late 1940's, Frankie Vaughan.

Born Frank Abelson in Liverpool, Frankie Vaughan was as well known for his stage costumes as his singing. With a top hat, tails, a bow tie and swishing a walking cane, he was the embodiment of the Fred Astaire song "Top Hat, White Tie and Tails". He successfully made the transition from a variety song and dance act to become a recording artist in 1950 but it was not until 1953 that he made the UK charts with a cover of the Guy Mitchell song "Istanbul (Not Constantinople)"

Frankie Vaughan's breakthrough came with what is regarded as his signature tune "Give Me the Moonlight, Give Me the Girl" in 1955 with which he would always close his concert appearances, but his biggest successes in the 1950's were also cover versions, this time of the Jim Lowe hit "Green Door" in 1956, which reached number 2 in the UK charts in November, 1956 and the Joe Valino record "The Garden of Eden", which hit the number 1 spot in January, 1957.

But it was a young American white singer called Elvis Aaron Presley who had begun his domination of the rock 'n' roll scene, captured the headlines and became the absolute symbol of rock 'n' roll. Teenagers all over Britain were practicing his lip curling, his hip shaking and doing their best to look and sound like Elvis…

Chapter Two: Britain's answer(s) to Elvis

"While the singer moves around like an Elvis clone"
(Al Stewart – Class of '58)

A truck driver from Memphis, Elvis seemed to embody the rhythm and soul of black musicians such as Little Richard and combined this rawness with a solid country and western swing to produce a sound that was as gripping as it was new.

But as much as British youth embraced Elvis and the other American rock 'n' rollers, there was an underlying feeling that perhaps Britain could do just as well, and the search was on for Britain's answer to Elvis, a local hero who could show those Yanks. And where would that search be concentrated? In the coffee bars, where skiffle still held sway, that's where.

The tradition of drinking coffee in convivial surroundings goes back to the establishment in 1691 of the Lloyd's coffee house in Tower Street, London, where merchants and ship owners would meet to discuss insurance deals.

The unlikely trigger for the modern coffee bar boom in England, however, was the arrival of the Gaggia espresso coffee machine from Italy in 1952. This machine was imported by the Italian actress and film star Gina Lollobrigida, who is credited with setting up of the first coffee bar – the Moka Espresso Bar at 29, Frith Street in London's West End.

The concept of the coffee bar quickly caught on and soon coffee bars were sprouting up over the country by entrepreneurs hoping to cash in on the new fad. One of the many coffee bars in the West End was the 2 I's Coffee Bar at 59, Old Compton Street, named after Freddy and Sammy Irani, the two brothers that ran it.

However, many would-be millionaires soon discovered that simply selling cups of cappuccino or espresso coffee was not as profitable as they thought and were forced to find other means of enticing clients to their establishments, such as serving food or – more importantly for would be musicians – offering live music to patrons.

The 2 I's faced stern competition from the many coffee bars in the immediate area, but when it was taken over in April, 1956 by two Australian wrestlers, Paul "Dr. Death" Lincoln and Ray "Rebel" Hunter, they realized that they must make their coffee bar stand out from the others around them if they were to succeed.

Agreeing that live music would attract more customers, they invited The Vipers skiffle group – an amateur but skilful group formed by a Londoner, Wallace 'Wally' Whyton – to play at their club on a regular basis after the group had called in for coffee during the Soho Fair parade in 1956.

One of the occasional members of The Vipers was a slim, blond-haired Thomas William Hicks, soon to be known to English fans as Tommy Steele.

Tommy Steele – let's use his stage name – was born in Bermondsey, south London on 17th December 1936. He failed his medical examination for call up to National Service, according to some sources because of a diagnosis of cardiomyopathy, but according to Tommy's autobiography, *Bermondsey Boy: Memories of a Forgotten World*, the reason was his flat feet.

Whatever the reason, Tommy pursued a number of short term jobs before signing on as a merchant seaman. Like so many of his contemporaries, Tommy began strumming on a guitar or banjo and soon graduated to performing in coffee bars around London both as a solo performer and occasionally as a member of the Vipers skiffle group. The line up of The Vipers was quite volatile, and fellow members of the group at various stages included not only Tommy Steele, but also Bruce Welch and Hank Marvin, both later to find fame in the backing group for Cliff Richard and later in their own right as one half of the chart-topping instrumental group The Shadows.

Figure 3 - Tommy Steele and The Steelmen
The Steelmen consisted of Dennis Price (Piano), Alan Stuart (Saxophone),
Leo Polloni (Drums) and Alan Weighell (Bass)
Photo courtesy of Barrie Smith

Life as a merchant seaman carried Tommy Steele across the Atlantic several times and on one occasion his ship landed in Norfolk, Virginia in the USA, where he was fascinated by the music of Buddy Holly. The impact of this charismatic performer on Tommy Steele cannot be over emphasized. The raw power and driving force of Holly's music convinced Tommy that the age of skiffle was over and that the future of popular music was rock 'n' roll.

Returning to England, Tommy Steele was soon fronting his own rock 'n' roll group, The Steelmen, taking the name from Tommy's stage name, which in turn Tommy had derived from the surname of his paternal Scandinavian grandfather, one Thomas Stil-Hicks.

At this time a freelance photographer and impresario, John Kennedy, was becoming interested in the burgeoning teenage music scene and was fascinated by stage performance and unique sound of Elvis Presley. What if, he mused, I could find an English equivalent to Elvis?

On a random visit to the 2 I's coffee bar in 1956, he thought he had found what he was looking for in The Steelmen. Seeing another Elvis on the stage, he arranged with his friend and associate Laurence Maurice Parnes, better known as Larry Parnes, to manage the group.

Laurence Parnes was born in Willesden in London in 1930. He started his working life in the clothing industry in Romford, in London's East End, but first became involved in show business when he became a partner in a bar in the West End of London, La Caverne in Romilly Street, Soho.

In 1954 Larry Parnes made an investment in a touring play called The House of Shame. A publicity stunt dreamed up by the play's publicist – one John Kennedy – to have two young girls dressed up as prostitutes stand outside the theatre in which the play was performed, gave the play a deal of notoriety and bolstered it's success.

Buoyed by the enthusiasm of John Kennedy, Larry Parnes could also see the potential of the young Tommy Steele and obtained a recording contract for The Steelmen with Decca. With thoughts of Elvis still in their minds, Parnes and Kennedy had The Steelmen record "Rock with the Caveman" as their first release in 1956 on September 24, 1956.

The song was co-written by Tommy Steele in partnership with a duo that was to create a river of hits for Tommy Steele and many others in the history of British popular music, Mike Pratt and Lionel Bart. Within a few weeks the record, backed by another rock 'n' roll song "Rock Around the Town", had entered the UK charts and within a month had reached number 13, facing stiff competition from the Americans Frankie Laine – with "A Woman in Love" – and Johnnie Ray, with his number 1 hit "Just Walkin' in the Rain".

There was to be no sitting back and resting on their laurels for The Steelmen and the Parnes/Kennedy/Bart/Pratt combination. The follow up single "Doomsday Rock" backed by "Elevator Rock" was quickly released but failed to reach the charts. Undeterred, the partners recorded and released "Singing the Blues" – a cover version of the American record by Guy Mitchell – backed with "Rebel Rock".

Despite the strong competition from the American record, The Steelmen's version reached number 1 in the UK charts on December 14, 1956. Over the next month the two versions competed against each other for the coveted number 1 position, with the Guy Mitchell version holding number 1 for a week early in January 1957, only to be replaced by the Steelmen for a week and then regain the top slot on January 18, 1957.

Such was the excitement generated by this young pretender to the Elvis throne that within four months of his initial UK chart success, Tommy was working on a film of his life, *The Tommy Steele Story*. The screenplay was written by Norman Kudis and called for a total of twelve songs. The song writing trio of Steele/Bart/Pratt managed this task in just seven days.

Tommy Steele continued to release records at a phenomenal rate over the next four years, enjoying chart success in 1957 with another Guy Mitchell cover "Knee Deep in the Blues" (number 15), "Butterfingers" (number 8), "Shiralee" (number 11), the double sided "A Handful of Songs/Water, Water" (number 5) and "Hey You" (number 28).

The success continued over 1958 with a further four chartings and two more in both 1959 and 1960, but his final chart success was the prophetically titled "The Writing on the Wall" which reached number 30 on August 17, 1961.

Although Tommy Steele was perhaps the first home-grown talent to score success in the world of rock 'n' roll, his overall persona seemed to lack the toughness, arrogance and the spirit of rebellion that the stars from America, such as Little Richard, Jerry Lee Lewis and of course Elvis, had in such abundance. Tommy was, unfortunately, seen as 'too nice' by the UK youth. What was needed was someone to capture that spirit, someone who could capture the menacing snarl, the quivering hips and the Elvis quiff.

With the success of Tommy Steele, the 2 I's coffee bar had struck gold. Young performers rushed to the venue in the hope of being discovered and put on the road to stardom.

One such likely candidate was a record packer, Terence Williams, who was convinced that he could produce the same energy and excitement on stage as his idols Elvis and Gene Vincent. Performing at the 2 I's coffee bar and producing a reasonable imitation of Gene Vincent, his potential impressed co-owner Paul Lincoln, who persuaded the music and TV producer Jack Good and Dick Rowe, the A&R manager from Decca records to sign him up and give him a recording contract.

The previous year the BBC, finally realizing that rock 'n' roll was not just a passing fad that would go away if ignored, had bowed to teenager pressure and had been persuaded to develop a TV program directed at the young.

The so-called 'Toddlers Truce' – a scheduling policy that no TV broadcasting should take place between the hours of 6pm and 7pm, to allow young children to be put to bed – had been abolished by Parliament with effect from Saturday, February 16, 1957.

This abolition left a blank in the BBC TV schedule, which they decided to fill with their new weekly program directed at teenagers. Because of the time slot now available, the program was called the *Six-Five Special* and was produced by Jack Good.

Jack Good had been impressed by the film *Rock Around the Clock*, not only by the music featuring among others Bill Haley and the Comets, but more by the audience reaction when the film was shown in British cinemas. The dancing in the aisles and the energy and excitement levels were what Good wanted to capture in a TV show.

From the outset, the BBC had requested a magazine format show, but Jack Good had other ideas – he realized that the teenagers wanted a vibrant and exciting show, representing the music that teenagers loved. Because of the limited recording abilities of the time, it was not possible to pre-record the show before broadcasting, so the show would go out live.

This gave Jack Good the opportunity to tailor the show the way he wanted. While he outwardly agreed with the BBC executives and had sets built representing the more stolid format, just before the show went on air the sets were cleared from the studio and replaced by just the audience and the performers.

The show was an immediate success, despite – or possibly because of – it's somewhat impromptu format. Among the local stars appearing on the show were Tommy Steele, skiffle legend Lonnie Donegan and jazz musician Humphrey Lyttleton.

Jack Good could see that Terence Williams, now to be known as Terry Dene, would provide an impetus to his *Six-Five Special* TV show and arranged for him to appear on the show.

Dick Rowe at Decca had also been busy and Terry Dene's first record "A White Sport Coat" – as usual for the times a cover version of an American hit, this time the original was written and recorded by Marty Robbins – reached number 18 in the UK charts on June 7, 1957. Dene's record faced stiff competition from the UK group The King Brothers, whose version had peaked at number 6 just a week previously.

Boosted by this successful entry into the UK charts, a second record – "Start Movin'" – was released almost immediately and also entered the charts, peaking at number 15 on July 19, 1957. However, these records failed to truly reflect the sounds that Terry Dene could produce on stage and although several other records followed, only one – "Stairway of Love" – figured in the charts, topping at number 18 in May, 1958.

Terry Dene's career was also impacted by adverse publicity when, following a drunken incident in which a shop window was broken, he was arrested for public drunkenness and branded as exemplifying "the evil of rock and roll" by a hostile press.

His fortunes were further shaken when he was called up for National Service in July, 1958, but this was deferred for two months to allow him to fulfil contractual obligations. His army career was short-lived however, as after just two months he was discharged on medical grounds after receiving threats from his fellow conscripts following the enormous publicity surrounding his conscription.

Larry Parnes was both encouraged by the success of Tommy Steele and The Steelmen and envious of the success of Terry Dene, and realized that he needed to find more performers to add to his entourage to fully realize the potential of the teenager market – a market still dominated in 1957 by Elvis, Buddy Holly, Little Richard and other powerful American stars.

Steele's co-writer on many of his hits, Lionel Bart, happened to be visiting the Condor Club in London in 1957, where he was impressed by the singer on stage, a certain Reg Patterson.

Bart shared his excitement with Larry Parnes, who was equally impressed with the young singer and saw the chance to promote him as 'the next Elvis' so he placed the youngster under contract and began the grooming process.

Born Reginald Leonard Smith in Blackheath, South London on April 15, 1939, the singer had started his career, like so many others, playing in a skiffle group, but had changed his name to Patterson before obtaining a residency at the Condor Club in 1957.

The first item on Parnes' agenda was the name. Reg Patterson certainly didn't have the same appeal as Elvis Presley or Chuck

Berry, so Parnes tried the trick of attempting to convey the singer's personality through his surname and changed Patterson to Wilde. Reg Wilde wasn't so hot either, but prompted by the success of the sentimental film *Marty* a couple of years back, Reg Wilde became Marty Wilde.

Marty Wilde was backed by The Wildcats, who at various incarnations of their existence included 'Big' Jim Sullivan[6] on lead guitar, Brian Bennett on drums and Brian Locking on bass, the latter two later went on to play in The Shadows with Hank Marvin and Bruce Welch.

Figure 4 - Vince Eager, Cliff Richard and Marty Wilde
Three cool cats, appearing on *Oh Boy!* in 1958
© Victoria and Albert Museum, London

Signed to Philips records, Marty Wilde followed the trusted and tried formula of producing cover versions of American records. In his case, his first single was a cover of the Jimmie Rodgers' "Honeycomb", which unfortunately failed to make the charts. His second single, "Sing, Boy, Sing" also failed to make any impact and things were looking bleak. However, Marty's third release, "Endless Sleep" – another cover version of a Jody Reynolds original – did much better and peaked at number 4 on the UK charts in July, 1958.

Marty Wilde made regular appearances on the Jack Good TV show the *Six-Five Special* which enhanced his appeal and helped promote his records. However, the BBC was not happy with the format of the show as promoted by Good and made more and more efforts to include educational snippets and educational segments in the program, ideas which were completely contrary to Good's concept of a full-on popular music showcase.

The bitterness between Jack Good and the BBC escalated to the extent that Good resigned early in 1958 and took his original concept to the relatively new commercial TV broadcaster, Independent Television, known then as ITV.

ITV welcomed Jack Good and his ideas and commissioned two pilot shows, which were broadcast only in the Midlands in June, 1958. Despite the limited audience, the pilots were well received and Good was given the go-ahead to produce a series of half-hour shows, to be called *Oh Boy!* and to be broadcast at 6pm on Saturdays – a direct competitor with Good's old program still showing on the BBC, but starting five minutes earlier.

The first show was broadcast on Saturday September 13, 1958 and among the performers starring in that first full episode was Marty Wilde. Others on the bill included Ronnie Carroll, The John Barry 7 and a certain Cliff Richard and his backing group The Drifters, who had just reached number 2 in the UK charts with "Move It".

The resident backing musicians were Lord Rockingham's X1 – although in fact the group had thirteen members. This group was formed by Jack Good and led by Harry Robinson and included such musical names as the baritone saxophonist and jazz writer Benny Green, organist Cherry Wainer and tenor saxophonist Red Price.

The group had a full, raucous sound and in addition to providing the backing for the singers and dancers on the show, recorded several instrumental tracks on the Decca label, one of which, "Hoots Mon" reached the coveted number 1 position on the UK charts in October, 1958.

Figure 5 - Jack Good and Lord Rockingham's XI
The crew at *Oh Boy!* In rehearsal. Jack Good (background) conducting Lord Rockingham's XI – with Cherry Wainer on keyboards – in 1958
© Victoria and Albert Museum, London

From the first nationwide program, *Oh Boy!* achieved a much greater popularity rating than the BBC's *Six-Five Special*, vindicating Jack Good's vision. Marty Wilde and Cliff Richard were both invited to appear on the second show the following week and Marty appeared on the third show the week after.

However, when Cliff Richard appeared once again on the fourth show on October 4, 1958, Larry Parnes became concerned at the rise in popularity and competition with his star, Marty Wilde, and headlines in the British music magazine, Melody Maker the next week announced that Marty Wilde had quit the *Oh Boy!* show, supposedly because he did not want to share top billing with Cliff.

Whether this is the true reason, or whether it was behind the scenes machinations by Parnes is unknown, but Marty Wilde was not among the performers to appear in the next edition of the show. He did, however return as a special guest sporadically over the rest of the year.

Larry Parnes had every reason to be concerned about the rise in popularity of Cliff Richard. His first record, produced by Norrie Paramor, featured a cover of the American record "Schoolboy Crush" by Bobby Helms, but it was the 'B' side, a straight out rock 'n' roll song called "Move It" which caught the attention of the record buying public.

Cliff Richard was born Harry Rodger Webb in Lucknow, India on October 14, 1940. Following Indian independence in 1948, the Webb family moved from relative affluence in India to a semi-detached house in Carshalton, Surrey, England and later in 1950 to Cheshunt in Hertfordshire, where young Harry Webb attended secondary school.

Like so many of his contemporaries – were there actually any youngsters of the time who weren't influenced by skiffle? – Harry became interested in popular music and after his father bought him his first guitar at age 15, he soon formed a vocal group named The Quintones, before moving on to join the Dick Teague Skiffle Group.

But the lure of rock 'n' roll tempted Harry and before long he was the front man and singer in a rock 'n' roll group, at the time called The Drifters. The other Drifters were Ian 'Sammy' Samwell and Norman Mitham playing guitars, while the drumming was the responsibility of Terry Smart.

The group was booked for their first real gig at the Regal Ballroom in Ripley, Derbyshire by entrepreneur Harry Greatorix, but he was not convinced that the name Harry Webb conveyed the right image for a rock 'n' roll singer. Searching for something more macho, Greatorix suggested Cliff – as in rock face – and Ian Samwell, a great admirer of Little Richard, suggested Richard as the new surname.

According to legend, Samwell rejected the idea of using 'Richards' as the surname, commenting that it should be 'Richard' without the 's' so that should someone refer to the young singer as Cliff Richards, they could be corrected, thus reinforcing the name by saying it twice.

Cliff Richard and The Drifters were signed to the EMI Columbia record label and were soon in the famous Studio Two in EMI's Abbey Road studios. Having chosen the 'A' side of the record as "Schoolboy Crush", producer Norrie Paramor looked for a suitable 'B' side. He didn't need to look far – Ian Samwell had recently composed his own tribute to rock 'n' roll which he titled "Move It" and suggested this as the 'B' side of the group's first record.

The song was composed by Samwell while travelling on the Number 715 Green Line bus service between Guildford and Hertford, via Shepherds Bush and Oxford Circus, on his way to Cliff's house for a rehearsal. The record was released on August 29, 1958

Paramor wanted to replicate the sound of the brash, American hit records, so he recruited two session musicians – Ernie Shears on guitar and Frank Clark on bass – to add to The Drifters sound.

Jack Good heard the record and immediately loved the 'B' side and wanted Cliff and The Drifters to perform it on his *Oh Boy!* TV show. Despite Paramor's protestations that "Schoolboy Crush" was the 'A' side, his teenage daughter sided with Jack Good and so it was that "Move It" was performed on *Oh Boy!* and became Cliff Richard's first UK chart success.

Many – not least a certain John Lennon – consider that "Move It" was the first real British rock 'n' roll record. Certainly the guitar intro still sends shivers up and down the spine and the driving beat propels the song forwards relentlessly.

The song, together with Cliff's performance on *Oh Boy!*, ensured that he became a regular on the program for the rest of 1958 and into 1959 and a firm favourite with teenagers in Britain. A string of hit records followed, with his second single, "High Class Baby" reaching number 7 on the UK charts. Cliff's third single, "Livin' Lovin' Doll" only made it to number 20, but "Mean Streak" bettered this with a high of number 20 before Cliff Richard finally reached number 1 in the UK charts with his fifth single "Living Doll" in July, 1959.

After this breakthrough, Cliff Richard's backing group The Drifters were forced to change their name after a legal challenge by the American group of the same name. The Drifters became The Shadows and it was as Cliff Richard and The Shadows that the combination recorded in the future. The first record under the new name was the easy listening "Travelling Light", which also reached number 1.

Although in the initial stages of his career Cliff favoured the Elvis quiff hairstyle and pelvic gyrations, he soon calmed down his act to present a more clean-cut image and broadened his repertoire by starring in a range of films aimed at the teenage market. Although his first film *Expresso Bongo* gave him a more dramatic role, like Elvis Presley in the States, his films, such as *The Young Ones* and *Summer Holiday* soon became vehicles to show off his vocal talents. The title songs from these movies also gave him chart success, with both reaching number 1.

Although by this time Britain's love affair with skiffle was beginning to wane, the 2 I's coffee bar was still the place to be seen and perhaps be discovered. Or so hoped a young film cutter named Terence Nelhams-Wright, who in his spare time dreamed of becoming a musician or actor.

Terence was a member of The Worried Men skiffle group, who had become the resident band at the 2 I's coffee bar. After being spotted by Jack Good, the group was given a spot on the *Six-Five Special* TV show, which so impressed Good that he offered Terence, the singer with the group, a solo recording contract with HMV, to be signed under the name Adam Faith.

Adam Faith's first record, "(Got a) Heartsick Feeling", released in January, 1958 failed miserably, as did his second release, a cover of the Jerry Lee Lewis hit "High School Confidential".

Figure 6 - Adam Faith
Adam Faith onstage at the NME Poll Winners Concert, Wembley, 1960
© Victoria and Albert Museum, London

Disheartened, Adam Faith returned to his day job as a film cutter at the National Film Studios at Elstree, but in March, 1959 fellow performer on The Six-Five Special, John Barry, of the John Barry Seven, invited him to appear in a new BBC TV music show called *Drumbeat*.

Torn between his secure job at Elstree and the lure of stardom, Adam Faith resigned his day job and became a regular on the show. Through his association with John Barry, Barry's manager, Eve Taylor, obtained a recording contract with Top Rank records, but once again his only recording for the label, "Ah, Poor Little Baby" sank without trace.

Adam's acting aspirations received a boost, however, when he was offered a role in a TV police drama, called *No Hiding Place*. But before he could take up the offer, his career prospects took another turn for the better. His friend John Barry was working on the score for a new adult musical film to be called *Beat Girl* and Adam Faith was offered a role. Through John Barry's contacts Adam was also offered a new recording contract with Columbia records on the Parlophone label and was soon in the famous Number 2 studio in Abbey Road, previously used by Cliff Richard to record "Move It".

The magic of that special studio seemed to rub off on Adam Faith and his particularly quirky vocal mannerisms, coupled with the original arrangement conjured up by Barry on the song "What Do You Want" quickly propelled him and the song to stardom as a serious rival to Cliff Richard. The song first entered the charts at number 18, but by the middle of November, 1959 it had reached number 1, where it stayed for the rest of the year.

The follow-up, again arranged by John Barry and titled "Poor Me" also reached number 1 in January, 1960 and over the year Adam Faith recorded a further four top ten hits.

Like Tommy Steele before him, and his contemporaries Marty Wilde and Cliff Richard, Adam Faith moved away from his rock 'n' roll roots towards light entertainment, acting and films, leaving once again a gap in the search for that elusive Elvis clone.

But the successes of Tommy, Marty, Cliff and Adam, and to a lesser extent Terry Dene, convinced Larry Parnes that the stage was now set for the great first invasion of the UK charts by home-grown artists.

Preferably, if he had his way, all managed by Larry Parnes…

Chapter Three: The Larry Parnes Family

"Oooh-wah, now I'm on a package tour"
(Al Stewart – Class of '58)

Larry Parnes had a simple philosophy – find attractive young men that he could transform into marketable propositions aimed at the teenage record buying public. It helped if the young man in question could sing, of course, but looks and personality were equally important.

Once established in the teenage market, Parnes aimed to have his protégées become more all-round entertainers in the mould of Tommy Steele and Cliff Richard. With a collection of entertainers, he would be able to organize package tours covering the length and breadth of the British Isles, showcasing his own stable of stars.

It was not for nothing then that Larry Parnes was called the Svengali of Pop and dubbed "Mr. Larry Parnes, Shillings and Pence" by the pop music press for his uncanny ability to make money from his troupe of teenage musicians.

His next major signing was Ronald Wycherley, a youngster from Liverpool. Ronald grew up in the tough area of Dingle and as a youngster had suffered from rheumatic fever when aged six and again at sixteen, causing him to miss out on much of his schooling and which was to cause health problems later throughout his life.

After completing his basic schooling, he obtained a job in an engineering works before moving on to become a deck hand on the Formby, one of the many tug boats plying the River Mersey. Working in the docks area gave Ronald access to the latest records brought in from America by visiting sailors.

He had taken piano lessons at the age of ten and his parents fostered his musical interests by buying him a guitar when he was fourteen. Initially he was influenced by American country and western singers, but like so many others of the time he was drawn to skif-fle music and, having taught himself basic chords on his guitar, soon formed his own group. Applying the Liverpudlian style of humour, the group was called the Formby Sniffle Gloup.

Although enjoying performing, his main ambition was to become a songwriter and he spent many hours scribbling lyrics and chords in a notebook as he developed his own songs.

He was impressed by the movie *The Girl Can't Help It*, starring American rock 'n' rollers Little Richard and Eddie Cochran, and after a friend remarked that he looked like Eddie Cochran, he decided to make his own recording at the local Percy F. Phillip's recording studio.

In a fit of bravado, a tape of the session, consisting of four Elvis Presley songs and one of his own compositions, together with a photograph of himself was sent to Larry Parnes in London.

Parnes had already established himself as an impresario and successful manager through Tommy Steele and Marty Wilde and had organized a touring package show, starring Marty Wilde, which was due to play the Essoldo Theatre in Birkenhead on October 1, 1958.

Larry Parnes was impressed by the looks and singing talent shown on the demo tape and accompanying photo and asked Ronald to meet him backstage at the Essoldo. In Marty Wilde's dressing room, Parnes asked Ronald to sing a couple of songs to him.

Ronald responded with two of his own compositions – "Margo", written in honour of a local shop girl, and "Maybe Tomorrow", a strong ballad. Despite the poor acoustics in the dressing room, Parnes made an amazing offer – "If I say to you that you're going on stage in eight minutes, what would you say?"

The somewhat dazed Ronald agreed and after a quick rehearsal went on stage during the second half of the show. The audience response was magnificent and Parnes signed him up on the spot to appear on the remainder of the tour, starting with Manchester the next evening.

But, Parnes being Parnes, he couldn't send his latest star out on stage with a name like Ronald Wycherley. Young Ron had hoped to be able to appear under the name that he had previously used in his skiffle group days, Stean Wade, but Parnes was keen on names that represented the personality of the performer, and so the vibrant and exciting Ronald Wycherley became Billy Fury.

Within a matter of days Parnes had obtained a recording contract for Billy with Decca records and shortly after he was in the studios recording his own composition "Maybe Tomorrow", which was released on January 16, 1959.

Things were moving quickly for Billy Fury. On February 14, 1959 he made his first appearance on the Jack Good TV show *Oh Boy!* and two weeks later "Maybe Tomorrow" entered the charts at number 18. Despite several appearances on *Oh Boy!* during March, April and May, including the final show in the series on May 30, the record could not improve on its position and slipped back out of the charts.

However, Billy's second release, the other song that he had auditioned for Larry Parnes, "Margo", was released in June and reached number 28 in June, 1959.

His third and fourth releases failed to make the charts, but he scored again in March, 1960 with his own song "Colette" and went on to register an impressive top 40 hits up until 1966, including hits such as "Wondrous Place" and "Halfway to Paradise".

As with Tommy Steele, Cliff Richard and Adam Faith, Billy Fury also appeared in films, his most noticeable being a starring role in the 1962 musical *Play it Cool*, modelled after the Elvis Presley musical films of the time.

The success of Billy Fury prompted Larry Parnes to look more closely at areas outside his normal stamping ground of London, in particular Liverpool, Fury's home town. But rather than going to Liverpool, Liverpool came to him, in the shape of John Askew.

John Askew was born and raised in Liverpool and on leaving school gained an apprenticeship as a carpenter. Once qualified, he obtained a job on an ocean liner and, browsing through a DIY book from the ship's library, he found plans for making a guitar.

Using his carpentry skills, John was able to complete the project in three months and then spent the rest of his non-working hours learning how to play it. He could often be found playing and singing as he composed his own songs and passengers on the liner urged him to take up singing on a professional basis.

At the end of that particular cruise, he took their advice and began entering talent shows, changing his stage name to firstly George Baker and then to the more American sounding Ricky Damone. However, the name changes did not bring him luck and he soon moved down to London where he hoped there was more scope for success.

Finding work on a building site, he continued to enter talent contests and finally won a competition held at the Locarno Ballroom in Streatham, South London. Handling the auditions for the contest was none other than Larry Parnes, who quickly saw the potential in the young singer. As usual, Parnes arranged for a new name and shortly after Johnny Gentle – named after his more refined singing style – was given a recording contract with Philips Records in 1959.

As was the case with Billy Fury, Johnny Gentle's first record release was a self-composed song called "Wendy", written while on the cruise liner. The record failed to make the charts, as did his second release "Milk From The Coconut".

Undeterred by the lack of chart success, Larry Parnes proposed a short tour of Scotland for Johnny Gentle in May, 1960. The problem was that the singer had no backing group for the tour.

Parnes was promoting a show in Liverpool early that month, starring Gene Vincent and supported by local groups Cass and The Casanovas, Gerry and The Pacemakers and Rory Storm and The Hurricanes, and proposed that he audition several Liverpool groups while in Liverpool for both the Scottish tour and a proposed tour of the north of England by Billy Fury.

Several groups attended the auditions on May 10, 1960, held at what is now the Blue Angel Club, formerly the Wyvern Social Club, on Seel Street in Liverpool. Among the groups were Derry and The Seniors, Cliff Roberts and The Rockers, Cass and the Casanovas and The Silver Beetles.

The Silver Beetles at that time included John Lennon, Paul McCartney, George Harrison, Stuart Sutcliffe and a drummer named Tommy Moore, who unfortunately didn't turn up for the audition, so Alan Williams, the Silver Beetles manager, sat in on drums.

With no regular drummer and Stuart Sutcliffe on bass out of his depth, the Silver Beetles failed the Billy Fury tour audition – but the call came from Parnes on May 18 that they had been selected to back Johnny Gentle on his brief Scottish tour, starting on May 20 at Alloa.

There was no time for full rehearsals – in fact Johnny Gentle only met the Silver Beetles just a half hour before the first show in Alloa – but despite this the two acts performed well together. So much so that when Johnny Gentle next needed a backup band on tour, he requested the Silver Beetles, but it was too late – the group were too busy writing history in Hamburg, Germany.

The 2 I's coffee bar was, as we have seen, the launching pad for the careers of many artists during the period of the late 1950's and it was here that Larry Parnes spotted yet another performer to add to his growing stable.

The musical career of Vince Eager – born Roy Taylor on June 4, 1940 in Grantham, Lincolnshire – began when at age 14 he formed a group with two friends which they called The Harmonica Vagabonds.

With the skiffle craze sweeping the country, the group quickly changed its name to The Vagabonds Skiffle Group and grew into a four-piece band. They gained local fame and notoriety in the clubs and dance halls around Grantham. Encouraged by their success, the Vagabonds optimistically entered the rather grandly named World Skiffle Championships.

Against all odds the group won a place in the final, televised by the BBC as a segment in the popular *Come Dancing* programme. They were not totally disappointed by the final judging – no fairy tale ending, but a second placing was enough for the group to be offered a resident stint at the 2 I's.

After being spotted by Larry Parnes on one of his visits to the 2 I's, the group was booked for a Sunday concert promoted by Parnes. The success of this concert lead till a tour and the release of an EP record under the name of Vince Eager and The Vagabonds.

Another consequence was two of The Vagabonds, Roy Clark and Mick Fretwell returning home to Grantham while the remaining Vagabond, Brian 'Liquorice' Locking joined Marty Wilde's backing group, The Wildcats, and later went on to find fame when he joined Cliff Richard's backing group The Shadows.

While Vince Eager was not a commercial success on record – he released ten singles in addition to his first EP between 1958 and 1963 on various record labels, starting with Parlophone, then Top Rank and finally Pye – he was a regular and strong performer on TV shows such as *The Six-Five Special, Oh Boy!* and *Drumbeat*. He toured with many of the top musical artists of the time, including Gene Vincent, Marty Wilde, Billy Fury and Jerry Lee Lewis, but it was the friendship that he developed with the American rock star Eddie Cochran which led to a rift with Larry Parnes and their eventual parting of the ways.

On January 24, 1960 the latest Larry Parnes promotion, "The Larry Parnes Fast Moving Beat Show" package tour, starring the American artists Gene Vincent and Eddie Cochran and including a variety of British artists from the Parnes stable, started what was scheduled as a twelve-week tour of Britain at the Gaumont Theatre, Ipswich in East Anglia.

The British acts on the tour varied from time to time as other commitments conflicted with the tour dates, but among the British stars who appeared at some stage during the tour were Billy Fury, Joe Brown, The Tony Sheridan Trio, Johnny Gentle and Vince Eager.

The success of the tour caused Parnes to add further dates, so that it was April 16 before the final show was performed, at the Bristol Hippodrome in the west of England. Eddie Cochran had a plane ticket to fly home to America from Heathrow airport at 1:00pm the next day and was keen to return to London after the show to avoid any possible delays.

The show finished late, well after the last train to London, so Eddie Cochran and Gene Vincent arranged for a taxi to take them back to London to collect some personal items before the flight.

The taxi ride ended in tragedy at an underpass near Chippenham, when the car spun out of control and slid backwards into a concrete lamp post. An ambulance was called and Eddie Cochran, who had been thrown from the car during the impact, was taken to St. Martin's hospital in nearby Bath suffering traumatic head and chest injuries.

Despite all the efforts of the medical staff, Eddie Cochran was pronounced dead at 4:10pm on Sunday April 17, 1960.

Larry Parnes rang Vince Eager early that Sunday to tell him of the accident and suggested Eager should go to the hospital, as Cochran was on the danger list at that time. Vince travelled to the hospital, where he was told by the attending surgeon that Cochran was unlikely to survive.

Devastated by the news, Vince left the hospital, only to find Larry Parnes holding a press conference on the steps outside, where the promoter announced – even before Cochran was pronounced dead

– that the American singer's next single would be called, prophetically, "Three Steps to Heaven".

This blatant publicity seeking disgusted Vince Eager and he immediately began steps to break away from the Parnes stable. A further reason to leave Parnes was the fact that he never seemed to receive any royalty payments from Parnes. When Eager queried this, Parnes reputedly told him "I have power of attorney over you, and I've decided you're not getting any".

With his contract seemingly water tight, Vince Eager had only one option, to refuse to work for Parnes until his contract expired in four years time – and this is pretty much what he did

Following the acrimonious split from Parnes, Vince Eager made the transition to a successful cabaret artist and played the mature Elvis Presley in Sir Laurence Olivier's West End musical stage play *Elvis* for five years.

Not all of Larry Parnes' signings were able to expand their career to become all round entertainers in the mould of Tommy Steele or Billy Fury. The case of Dickie Pride reveals a darker aspect of the pop world of those times.

Dickie Pride started life in October, 1941 as Richard Charles Knellar. He was gifted with a fine voice and as a youngster won a scholarship to the Croydon Royal College of Church Music. However, like so many other youngsters of the time, his musical preferences were towards music of the popular variety and he soon formed a skiffle group called The Semi-Tones.

The group performed locally in the Croydon area of South London and it was during one of these gigs at the Castle public house in Tooting that he was spotted by the piano player Russ Conway – who himself would go on to have several chart successes in 1959 and 1960.

Conway recommended the young singer – still only 16 at this time – to Larry Parnes, who saw his potential as a rock 'n' roll star, signed him up and – you've guessed it – changed his name to Dickie Pride.

Dickie's first gig was at the largest cinema in the country at the time – the Kilburn Gaumont – but the young Dickie was certainly not overawed by his surroundings. He made the transition from the local pubs to a massive theatre with ease and, as the Record Mirror reported in its review "he ripped it up from the start" and gained the nickname the Sheik of Shake.

After several more concert appearances and a guest spot on Jack Good's *Oh Boy!* TV show in February, 1959, his status as a Parnes protégé was confirmed when he obtained a recording contract with Columbia records to record with the highly successful producer Norrie Paramor.

Dickie's first single, released in March, 1959 was a cover version of the Little Richard hit "Slippin' and Slidin'" but this unfortunately failed to capture the excitement of his live performances and failed to reach the charts, despite several more appearances on *Oh Boy!*

A second attempt was made with the ballad "Primrose Lane" backed with a rock 'n' roll song "Frantic". Unusually, it was the ballad that entered the charts, peaking at number 28 on October 30, 1959 but the record only stayed in the charts for one week and was to prove to be Dickie Pride's only charting record.

Sadly, Dickie Pride could never transfer the vibrancy of his concerts to records. While he performed successfully on TV and on tour, his recording career came to end with an attempt by Larry Parnes to market him as a mainstream, rather than rock 'n' roll singer in 1961 with the release of the LP *Pride With Prejudice* containing standards and with Dickie performing with The Eric Jupp Orchestra.

The record failed to achieve the hoped for success and Dickie Pride was released from his contract with Parnes. Over the following years Dickie suffered from mental health problems and drug addiction until in 1967 he was admitted to a psychiatric clinic.

Dickie Pride took an overdose of sleeping pills and was found dead in his bed on March 26, 1969. He was not the only one of the Larry Parnes entourage to suffer from mental health problems, but the case of Duffy Power has a happier ending.

Larry Parnes was in the habit of visiting talent shows and competitions as often as he could manage, in the hope of discovering more promising youngsters he could mould into successful performers for his stable.

One such visit took place in early 1959, to a theatre in South West London, where he was impressed by a local group named Duffy and The Dreamers, fronted by 17-year old Raymond Howard who not only sang but played lead guitar under the stage name Duffy Howard.

Signing the young front man, Parnes renamed him as Duffy Power and arranged a recording contract with Fontana records. Despite Duffy's love of the more raw sounds of artists such as Ray Charles and Muddy Waters, his first records for Fontana were, in the main, covers of more easy listening styled songs by Bobby Darin and Bobby Rydell.

Songs such as "Dream Lover" and "Ain't She Sweet" failed to make the charts and even a cover version of the Jerry Lee Lewis classic "Whole Lotta Shakin' Goin' On" proved no commercial success.

Disappointed by the failure of his records, which he blamed on the poor choice of material selected by Larry Parnes, Duffy reasoned that he was unlikely to achieve success while still contracted to Parnes and split with his manager in late 1961.

But splitting from Parnes didn't improve matters – the excitement of the initial success of British grown rock 'n' roll was beginning to grow thin amongst the teenagers of the time. Duffy Power grew more and more depressed until finally he attempted suicide by gassing himself.

Fortunately he was rescued by a lucky call from a friend, who took Duffy to a local rhythm and blues club to recover. The music he heard there was a revelation and Duffy realized that his future must lie with the blues.

He joined forces with The Graham Bond Quartet, which at the time included both Jack Bruce and Ginger Baker – both later to form Cream with Eric Clapton – and the group's recording of the Lennon-McCartney classic "I Saw Her Standing There" in early 1963 is today considered a British milestone.

Having discovered his true direction musically, Duffy Power could be found later in the decade in the company of the illustrious blues legend Alexis Corner and despite fading from the music business during the 1970's and facing mental health problems, Duffy Power began to re-emerge in the 1980's and today is regarded as one of Britain's critically acclaimed rhythm and blues interpreters.

After Wilde, Fury, Eager, Pride and Power, it seemed likely that Larry Parnes might soon run out of surnames for his pop protégées but he still managed to come up with several more. One choice of name that caused some confusion was Lance Fortune.

In 1959 a sixteen year old Clive Powell, from Leigh in Lancashire was spotted playing piano and singing by Lionel Bart – co composer of many of the Tommy Steele songs – and recommended to Larry Parnes.

Parnes signed the young musician and offered him the stage name Lance Fortune. Unfortunately – or perhaps fortunately – Parnes had forgotten that he had already given the name to another of his recent signings, Christopher Morris, from Birkenhead in Cheshire.

Realizing his mistake, Parnes then decided on the stage name Georgie Fame for the young Clive Powell. Powell was not over-excited by his new name but, as he explained later in life, Parnes told him "If you don't use my name, I won't use you in my show". So the name stuck.

Georgie Fame spent most of his time on tour with assorted Larry Parnes packages, playing piano in the group appearing behind Billy Fury, The Blue Flames. However, as Billy Fury changed his style more and more to ballads, The Blue Flames more rock orientated style became less suited and eventually Billy Fury and The Blue Flames parted company at the end of 1961, leaving Georgie Fame to become the leader of the group and to have their own successes in the mid 1960's with records such as "Yeh Yeh" (1964), "Getaway" (1966) and "The Ballad Of Bonnie And Clyde" (1967), all of which reached number 1 in the UK charts.

The artist who ended up with the name Lance Fortune, Christopher Morris, was a classically trained pianist from Birkenhead in Liverpool who formed his first rock 'n' roll group – The Firecrests – while still at school.

Although he started at university after finishing his schooling, Chris Morris was soon drawn to London, decided to quit his university course and it was while performing at the 2 I's coffee bar that he was seen by Larry Parnes.

Parnes suggested the name Lance Fortune and managed to obtain a recording contract with Pye records for his discovery, although he never actually managed Fortune. His first record for Pye was "Be Mine", produced by Joe Meek. Backed by The John Barry Seven and in the style of Adam Faith, the record reached a creditable number 4 in the UK charts in 1960. A follow up, "This Love I Have For You", climbed into the UK top thirty, but thereafter Lance Fortune disappeared from the music scene as a solo artist.

A noticeable exception to the Parnes name-changing rule was a spiky-haired talented guitarist who, although born in Swarby, Lincolnshire, is rightfully regarded as a cockney as he moved to the East London suburb of Plaistow when he was just two years old.

With the given names of Joseph Roger Brown, you would assume that he was the ideal candidate for a Parnes-inspired name change, but the name Elmer Twitch, reputedly offered to Joe Brown by Larry Parnes, apparently did not go down too well, so Joe Brown he remained.

Figure 7 - Billy Fury and Joe Brown
Two of Larry Parnes' boys – Billy Fury – seen holding Joe Brown's Gibson ES355 guitar – and Joe himself.
© Victoria and Albert Museum, London

Despite his cockney cheerfulness and apparently easy-go-lucky attitude, Joe Brown was a master of the guitar and it was in 1958 while playing with his skiffle group, The Spacemen – which he had formed in 1956 – that he was spotted by the TV producer Jack Good and offered the position of lead guitarist in the house band for Good's new TV show *Boy Meets Girls*.

The new show was a successor to Good's previous show *Oh Boy!* and was intended as a showcase for Marty Wilde (the boy) and the all-girl singing group The Vernons Girls (the girls). The show kicked off in September, 1959 and ran for a total of 26 weekly episodes until closing in February, 1960.

Leading the house band gave Joe Brown ample opportunity to enhance his already formidable skills on guitar and after he had signed a management contract with Larry Parnes, he was called upon to provide backing for visiting American singers, such as Gene Vincent and Eddie Cochran, during their UK tours.

Although his first record, the 1959 title "People Gotta Talk" failed to chart, Joe's initial chart success came in March, 1960 when he and his group, The Bruvvers – which included two members of his original Spacemen skiffle group – reached number 34 in the UK charts with the "Darktown Strutters Ball". He gained chart success again later that year with "Shine" but it was in 1962 that he made his real breakthrough with the number two charting "A Picture of You".

Joe Brown was another of the Larry Parnes stable who successfully made the transition from rock 'n' roll singer to all-round entertainer and starred in the West End hit musical *Charlie Girl* from the opening night on December 15, 1965 until he left the show in 1968 – his replacement being one Gerry Marsden, of Gerry and The Pacemakers fame.

Perhaps the most convincing of the British answers to Elvis – although a little belated in his arrival – was Brian Maurice Holden. Born in Isleworth, in Middlesex, the Holden family migrated to America when Brian was just seven. There, in 1955, his sister married the American animator Joe Barbera, later to find fame as one half of the Hanna-Barbera television animation studios and responsible for the hugely successful Flintstones and Yogi Bear cartoon series.

After the marriage, the whole family moved west to California, where young Brian spent his teenage years studying, amongst other things, radio and meteorology. He also took flying lessons and obtained his pilots license while studying at Glendale School.

In 1957, like most teenagers of the time, he fell under the spell of rock 'n' roll, in particular Elvis Presley and Bill Haley and soon began singing at local school proms and parties. Encouraged by his reception, his brother-in-law Joe Barbera became his manager and when Barbera went to London on business shortly after, he invited Brian to accompany him to check out the music scene in England.

By August 1958 the pair had discovered the 2 I's coffee bar and during the month they approached the resident band, comprising Tony Meehan on drums, Tex Makins on bass and Tony Sheridan on guitar and asked if they were interested in becoming Brian's backing group, to be known as The Playboys.

The story goes that Brian, while idly flipping over a packet of cigarettes, saw the words "In hoc signo vinces" – which roughly translated from the Latin to "under this sign you will succeed". Brian took this as a good omen and decided to adopt the name Vince as his stage name. Feeling that perhaps Vince Holden didn't sound particularly showbiz, he then took on the surname of his favourite film actor, Robert Taylor, to become Vince Taylor.

Vince Taylor and The Playboys scored a record contract with Parlophone records and in November, 1958 released their first single "I Like Love" backed by "Right Behind You Baby". By this time the line-up of the Playboys had undergone several changes, with Tony Meehan – later to star in The Shadows – replaced by Brian Bennett – who in a curious coincidence would later replace Meehan in The Shadows. Other changes to the line-up included the addition of guitarist Tony Harvey and the replacement of Tex Makins on bass with Brian 'Liquorice' Locking – who would also make his way to The Shadows.

In one of those lucky breaks in show business, Vince Taylor and The Playboys were booked as last minute replacements for Cliff Richard at a show at the Regal Theater, Colchester, when Cliff had to withdraw due to a severe throat infection.

The group came to the attention of the TV producer Jack Good, who booked them to appear in his ITV show *Oh Boy!* in late 1958 and early 1959. Once again the line-up changed, as Tony Harvey left to join Clay Nicholls and his Blue Flames and, after an argument with Vince, Tony Sheridan left to form his own trio and was replaced by guitarist Joe Moretti.

It was not until April, 1959 that the group released their second and arguably most successful record, "Pledgin' My Love" backed by Vince's own composition "Brand New Cadillac".

Despite being banned by the BBC for the not so covert advertising of the brand name Cadillac, the 'B' side was the most successful and was recorded under the direction of Norrie Paramor, Cliff Richard's producer, and with scintillating lead guitar work by Joe Moretti – who would later provide top quality work on the Johnny Kidd and The Pirates later hit "Shakin' All Over" .

Cadillac has been recorded a number of times by other groups, including the Swedish group The Hep Stars – which featured a young Benny Andersson, later of ABBA, on piano – and later by The Clash on their classic 1979 album 'London Calling'.

Because of the BBC ban, sales of the record were limited and Parlophone responded by dropping the group soon after. Work was hard to come by and Joe Barbera left to return to California, convinced that his brother-in-law was not going to be an overnight success after all. The band split shortly after, Brian Locking and Brian Bennett heading to join Marty Wilde's backing group, The Wildcats, and Joe Moretti replacing Denny Wright in the country group Johnny Duncan's Blue Grass Boys before becoming a highly respected session guitarist.

Several reincarnations of The Playboys followed, including the addition of drummer Bobbie Woodman – also known as Bobbie Clarke – who had played with both Marty Wilde and Billy Fury and in July, 1961 Vince Taylor and His Playboys, as they were then known performed at the British Rock Festival at the Olympia Theater, Paris.

Taylor's performance there lead to a recording contract in France and he became perhaps an even bigger star in France than he had been in Britain, topping the bill at the Paris Olympia. However, more disagreements with the band ended with a fateful trip to London by Vince Taylor, supposedly to collect money owing to the band, but Taylor returned a different person after an encounter with the acid rock scene, claiming to be the prophet Mathew, the son of Jesus Christ.

And so the great British Elvis hunt came to an end, as fans across the country realized that there was, and could be, only one Elvis Presley. But the rock 'n' roll show must go on, even if it had been diluted and watered down from the excitement of the original...

Chapter Four: – But Wait – There's More!

"Then came the kid with the red Colorama"
(Al Stewart – Class of '58)

A casual observer of the British music scene during the few years between the mid 1950's and the early 1960's could be forgiven for thinking that a certain Larry Parnes owned the complete music scene.

While it is true that Larry Parnes was probably the most successful entrepreneur of the early British rock 'n' roll scene and had many acts under his control, the rock 'n' roll boom in the 1950's was not solely dependent upon Larry Parnes.

Once the initial breakthrough had been made by Tommy Steele, Marty Wilde and the other pioneers, the search was on for new faces to fill the ever growing demand for rock 'n' roll singers who had the looks – and maybe the talent – to appeal to the teenage market clamouring for more.

Television shows such as the *Six-Five Special* became the showcase for eager young British acts desperate to emulate the successes of their heroes.

The *Six-Five Special* was the first of the TV shows aimed at teenagers and initially focused on skiffle – the signature tune was performed by the Bob Cort Skiffle Group for the first few episodes, before Don Lang and His Frantic Five became the resident house band and performed the title song under the opening credits.

Although aimed at teenagers, the BBC vision for the show was anything but a rock 'n' roll programme. Instead the show was interspersed with 'educational and informative' segments, breaking the flow of the music.

Guest artists on the show included acts such as Jim Dale, who was in initially hired as a warm-up act before the show, but because of his popularity soon became a regular, singing such songs as "Piccadilly Line" – a send-up of the Lonnie Donegan hit "Rock Island Line". But he was also treated as a serious rock 'n' roll singer and in October, 1957 he reached number 2 on the UK charts with "Be My Girl".

Further records didn't fare so well, only reaching the lower end of the top thirty, but Jim Dale was another performer who extended his audience appeal into acting and is probably better known for his appearances in the *Carry On* series of British comedy films and for his composition of The Seekers hit song and movie theme "Georgy Girl" than for his pop singing career.

Another performer to get his break on the show was the man known to many as the singing milkman. Terry Perkins was invited to appear on the *Six-Five Special* after winning a talent contest and, despite appearing on the same bill as Cliff Richard and Joe Brown, his middle of the road stage style – neither too rock 'n' roll for the parents nor too soft for the teenagers – gave him instant success.

As was usual, he was persuaded to change his real name to become Craig Douglas – not by Larry Parnes this time, but by his manager Bunny Lewis, who noticed the name outside a house in Scotland. His success on the *Six-Five Special* earned Craig Douglas a recording contract with Decca, but after his first two records failed to make the charts, he was dropped by the label, but managed to obtain a second chance contract with the then newly formed Top Rank label.

His second Top Rank release, "Come Softly To Me" reached number 13 in the UK charts in June, 1959 and the follow up single "Only Sixteen", recorded in the EMI's Abbey Road studios, outsold the Sam Cooke version to become Craig's only chart topper in August the same year.

Craig Douglas went on to have several more chart successes over the next year and entered the 'Song for Europe' contest to find an entrant for Britain in the Eurovision Song Contest in 1961. Unfortunately Craig Douglas finished last in the contest, won by The Allisons with "Are You Sure".

To prove the variety aspect of the *Six-Five Special*, the BBC even had a professional boxer, Freddie Mills, appear regularly on the show as a presenter, although to be fair, Mills had enjoyed some success as a light entertainer during his stint in the Royal Air Force during the early 1940's.

But while the *Six-Five Special* – innovative as it was for its time – was a disappointment, its successor on the new ITV channel, produced by Jack Good and called *Oh Boy!* rapidly became required viewing for British teenagers.

Oh Boy! out performed the *Six-Five Special* in the ratings so much that the BBC closed down the latter shortly after *Oh Boy!* began broadcasting. However, many of the performers from the *Six-Five Special* did make appearances on the new show, including Don Lang.

But appearances on *Oh Boy!* were no guarantee for musical stardom. Take, for example, the case of Dudley Heslop who, under the stage name Cuddly Dudley, appeared no less than 21 times on the show, but still failed to register a UK chart success.

Billed as 'Britain's first black rock 'n' roller', Dudley was actually born in Kingston, Jamaica, before moving to Britain in his early twenties, where he spent some time singing in clubs and performing in variety shows.

He joined The Charles Ross Orchestra in the mid 1950's and it was then, because of his somewhat rotund figure, he gained the name Cuddly Dudley. He toured overseas with the Ross Orchestra before becoming interested in rock 'n' roll and his manager of the time decided to promote him as Britain's Big Bopper.

With his changed musical style came more expansive and flamboyant clothes and this brought him to the attention of producer Jack

Good, who signed him to appear in the first two pilot episodes of *Oh Boy!*, which aired in June, 1958. Dudley made such an impression that he appeared as a regular on the show, making his first appearance in the actual show in the second episode, which aired on September 20, 1958. Alongside him were Cliff Richard and the Drifters, The John Barry Seven and Marty Wilde.

But despite the success in the UK charts of black artists such as Nat 'King' Cole, Fats Domino and Little Richard, home grown black rock 'n' roll acts were very much in the minority. Another of the few such acts was the group Neville Taylor and The Cutters.

Born in the West Indies, Neville Taylor modelled his rock 'n' roll singing very much on the Little Richard style, but he was also a very convincing ballad singer. He and his group The Cutters made several appearances on *Oh Boy!*, but, despite this exposure they, like Cuddly Dudley, made little impact on the UK charts, although both acts appeared on the *Oh Boy!* LP released in 1958.

Yet another performer who originated from the West Indies was Emile Ford. Born in St. Lucia, Michael Emile Telford Miller had an unusual condition known as synesthesia, which enabled him to visualize sound as a series of colours and patterns. This in turn fired his interest in sounds and particularly music and was the main reason for him to move to London in the mid 1950's.

He attended the Paddington Technical College in London and because of his extreme interest in high quality sound recording techniques, taught himself to play a range of musical instruments, including piano and guitar and eventually formed a group with his half brother George (his mother had previously remarried), Ken Street (electric guitar) and drummer John Cuffley, which they called Emile Ford and The Checkmates.

With several amateur appearances behind them, the group eventually won the Soho Fair talent contest in July, 1959 but, when offered a recording contract with EMI, turned it down as the company would not allow Emile to produce his own records. Instead, they signed with Pye records, where they were allowed greater control in the studios.

The group's first record, under their own production control, was a cover of the original 1917 hit "What Do You Want To Make Those Eyes At Me For?" by Ada Jones and Billy Murray. This first single, although originally destined to be the B side for "Don't Tell Me Your Troubles" hit the top of the UK charts in October, 1959 and repeated the feat in December the same year when it stayed in the number 1 position for six weeks. The song, coincidentally has the honour of being the first record by a black British artist to sell over one million copies – and is also listed as the longest ever question asked by a number 1 record in the UK.

Not all performers making the British charts came from so far afield as the West Indies – several local performers also featured on those early TV music shows produced by Jack Good. Much closer to home, Bermondsey was the birthplace of the man who soon became known as Britain's wild man of rock 'n' roll – Wee Willie Harris.

Charles William Harris was born in Bermondsey, south London and, after spending some time working as a pudding mixer in one of London's bakeries, understandably decided that becoming a professional musician was a much more attractive proposition.

He began his career – as so many others – at the 2 I's coffee bar in Soho, where he was the resident piano player, providing backup to the many performers who passed through that establishment, such as Tommy Steele and Adam Faith. Because of his short stature – just 5' 2" tall – he became known as Wee Willie Harris.

Some sources claim that Wee Willie Harris was the pianist and vocalist featured in The Rockets on the Tony Crombie and The Rockets record of "(We're Goin' To) Teach You To Rock", although this cannot be substantiated.

Discovered – again like so many others – by Jack Good, Harris was offered a spot on the *Six-Five Special* TV show in November,

1957. His wild on stage antics caused consternation among newspaper critics, one of whom described his performance as being likened to "an exploding Catherine wheel, emitting growls, squeals and what sounds like severe hiccupping."

Certainly Wee Willie Harris was not one to go unnoticed on stage – he frequently died his hair green – or orange or perhaps pink – and wore jackets with heavy shoulder pads, tight drainpipe trousers and an enormous bow tie.

On his first solo record, released in 1957, Harris paid tribute to his musical origins with "Rockin' at the Two I's", but despite a string of releases on the Decca label in 1957 and 1958, he remained much more popular as a live performer than as a recording artist, and never hit the UK charts.

He continued to perform through the 1960's and 1970's, supporting several big name overseas acts such as Conway Twitty, Johnny Preston and Freddie Cannon and as late as 2003 released the album "Rag Moppin'".

A performer who attained legendary status – perhaps more by association than his own efforts – was Tony Sheridan.

Born slightly further afield – Norwich, Norfolk – than the Bermondsey of Wee Willie Harris, Anthony Esmond Sheridan McGinnity learned to play the violin as a young boy, influenced by his classical music loving parents.

He soon moved on to the guitar and formed his first band in 1956. He drifted in to London and eventually found himself playing guitar at the 2 I's coffee bar – where else? – for a mere pittance that left him sleeping on the streets. Spotted while playing at the 2 I's, Sheridan was soon making appearances in the *Oh Boy!* TV show during March, April and May, 1959.

As a result of these appearances, Tony Sheridan was booked by Larry Parnes to make some appearances in his package tour – a Fast

Moving Beat Show – starring the American acts Gene Vincent and Eddie Cochran. It was after the final performance of this tour, at the Bristol Hippodrome, that Tony Sheridan attempted unsuccessfully to get a lift to London in the taxi carrying the two American stars.

History records that the taxi crashed on the way to London just outside Bath, killing Eddie Cochran and seriously injuring Gene Vincent.

While gaining some degree of success, Sheridan also gained a reputation as being unreliable, and for turning up late for gigs, sometimes minus his guitar. Finding work harder to come by in England, Sheridan managed to get a booking at the infamous Kaiserkeller club in Hamburg.

During his stint in Hamburg between 1960 and 1963, Sheridan would use whatever musicians he could find to play behind him. In 1961 he became particularly friendly with a young group from Liverpool playing at the Indra club just down the road, often using them as his backup band and just as often sitting in with the group during their set.

The German record producer and A&R manager for Polydor records, Bert Kaempfert, happened to catch on of the joint performances and suggested that the combined acts should make a record together, although as far as he was concerned, the one with the most potential was Tony Sheridan.

Seven tracks were recorded over the two day session – five featuring Tony Sheridan and the backup group and just two with only the backup group alone – in June, 1961.

In 1962 Polydor records released the first single in Germany from the session – a combination of "My Bonnie" backed with "The Saints" under the label Tony Sheridan and The Beat Brothers. Apparently the backing group's stage name, The Beatles, sounded uncomfortably like the Hamburg slang term for the plural of penis.

However for UK release the record label correctly gave credit to Tony Sheridan and The Beatles.

Although the *Six-Five Special* and *Oh Boy!* were the first TV shows aimed specifically at the emerging teenage market, the BBC had tried various format music TV shows prior to these ground-breaking programmes. In 1952 they started the show *Hit Parade* – a cover of the successful American series called *Your Hit Parade*, but rather than have the original artists perform their hit records – far too expensive and impossible to bring over American artists – the songs were "interpreted" by a team of dancers with occasional performances by a team of resident singers, which included Denis Lotis and Petula Clark.

The show didn't last long, but was revived in October, 1955, probably in response to the newly launched ITV network, and the new series ran until August, 1956.

But it was not just in Britain that TV was seen as a way of in-creasing musical content for viewers. As Europe continued to rebuild after the Second World War, the concept of the Eurovision Song Contest was launched in Switzerland, when the European Broadcasting Union came up with the idea of linking member countries with a live broadcast light entertainment programme in which each country sub-mitted a "Song for Europe".

The contest was initially known as the Eurovision Grand Prix as was based on the San Remo song contest held in Italy. The concept was daring for an age without satellite linkages – all international communications then was handled by microwave links – but the first contest was scheduled to be held in Lugarno, Switzerland, on May 24, 1956.

That first contest only attracted seven countries – the Nether-lands, France, Germany, Luxembourg, Belgium, Italy and the host country Switzerland – and was won by Switzerland. For the first year, each participating country submitted two songs, a practice which was changed for subsequent years to allow only one song per country.

Britain first entered the following year, with the song "All", performed by Patricia Bredin, but finished a lowly seventh of the ten countries that entered. The UK declined to enter in the 1958 contest, held in Hilversum, in the Netherlands, but in 1959, when the contest was held in Cannes, France, the husband and wife team of Pearl Carr and Teddy Johnson came second with the song "Sing Little Birdie".

In 1960, France declined to host the competition, citing financial problems, so the contest was held in London. Competing that year for Britain was the singer Bryan Johnson – no relation to Teddy – who again came home in second place with the song "Looking High, High, High."

In 1961 the contest returned to the French city of Cannes, and this time the UK entry was the pop duo named The Allisons, a close harmony pair that resembled the Everly Brothers and The Kalin Twins, who had achieved a number 1 UK hit in 1958 with their song "When".

The Allisons, although marketed as the brothers John and Bob, were in fact ex-choir boys from Parsons Green in Fulham, west London named Brian Alford (John Allison) and Colin Day (Bob Allison).

Brian Alford had started his singing career when he formed his own skiffle group in 1956 which he called The Shadows – not to be confused with the instrumental group of the same name. In 1958 Alford and a fellow Shadow, John White, formed a singing partnership called The Shadows Brothers – a portent of things to come – and entered a national TV talent competition, the *Carroll Levis Television Discoveries.*

However, the duo's two appearances on this show, although giving them some exposure, did not attract sufficient attention to convince John White that the duo had a future in show business, and he decided to quit in January, 1959, leaving Brian Alford to continue as a solo performer.

In August that year, Alford once again joined forces with his former choir boy mate, Colin Day, and changed their performing name to The Allisons, thinking this sounded more professional and would enhance their image as 'brothers'.

Singing together, the pair had managed to establish themselves as the resident singers at the Breadbasket coffee bar in Cleveland Street, London – where previous talents had included Wally Whyton, Emile Ford and Jimmy Justice.

The pair entered yet another national talent show, sponsored by the pop musical newspaper DISC, which they won, with the prize being a national TV appearance on the Bert Weedon programme *Lucky Dip* together with a recording test with Fontana records.

The duo sang several of Alford's own compositions from 1957 and 1958, including the song "Are You Sure". Fontana records were so impressed by this song that they selected it to appear in the heats of the competition to decide the UK's entry for that year's Eurovision Song Contest.

The song won the UK heats with a runaway victory and the pair performed the song in Cannes in 1961 with high hopes of success, but once again the UK ended in second place. The record was successful in the UK charts, reaching number 2 in February, 1961, but further releases by The Allisons performed poorly and the pair split in the mid 1960's.

Unlike The Allisons, The Brook Brothers were real brothers and at one stage were dubbed 'Britain's Everly Brothers' although in reality they never achieved the heights in chart success that their American counterparts did.

Ricky and Geoffrey Brook, as with so many other youngsters in Britain, started their musical journey as members of a skiffle group but after finding success as winners of a TV talent show, decided to model themselves on the Everly Brothers.

The brothers secured a recording contract with Top Rank records and their first single, a cover of the American folk singing group The Brothers Four, "Greenfields" was released in 1960 and despite achieving chart success in Italy, failed to have any impact in the UK.

A second single released through Top Rank, very much under the Everly Brothers influence, called "Please Help Me I'm Fallin'" backed by a cover of the Everly's own "When Will I Be Loved" also failed miserably.

However, the duo switched to Pye records, where they were fortunate to come under the auspices of record producer/songwriter Tony Hatch. After a forgettable debut Pye single, "Say The Word", the brothers finally hit the mark with their recording of the Howard Greenfield and Bobby Mann song "Warpaint", which reached number 5 in the UK charts in April, 1961.

After a small glitch with their next release, "Little Bitty Heart", which failed to chart, the Tony Hatch magic was at work again on their recording of "Ain't Gonna Wash For A Week", which gave them another chart success when it peaked at number 13 in the UK charts later the same year.

However, their popularity had begun to fade, despite touring nationally with Cliff Richard and Bobby Rydell and an appearance in the Richard Lester produced musical film *It's Trad Dad,* and hits became harder to find. Their last chart success was in 1963, when they reached number 38 in the UK charts with "Trouble Is My Middle Name" and thereafter they succumbed to the onslaught of the beat boom.

Not satisfied with the show *Hit Parade,* The BBC made another attempt to satisfy the younger audience when it launched *Off The Record* in May, 1955. This was a mixture of pop music news, interviews and live performers, both British and visiting American stars. The first programme in the series included Alma Cogan, Max Bygraves and Ronnie Hilton – hardly the stuff of which rock 'n' roll dreams are made – but before the show closed in March, 1958 it had scored a major coup with a live performance of "Maybe Baby" by Buddy Holly and The Crickets during their 1958 UK tour.

The first serious attempt to corner the rock 'n' roll television audience was the Associated Rediffusion show *Cool For Cats*, which was first broadcast on December 31, 1956. Initially just fifteen minutes long, the show was extended to a thirty minute format each Thursday evening at 7:15pm, but by June, 1957 it had increased to twice weekly. The long term presenter was Kent Walton, better known for his work on Radio Luxembourg and the format was similar to that of the earlier BBC *Hit Parade*, with very few live rock 'n' roll performances.

However, by the end of the 1950's it had become passé with the advent of the *Six-Five Special* and *Oh Boy!* and was quietly shelved in February, 1961.

When the *Six-Five Special* was dropped in January, 1959, beaten by *Oh Boy!* in the popularity stakes, the BBC tried yet another show, this time called *Dig This!* but again the BBC show was overwhelmed by the ITV's *Oh Boy!* and *Dig This!* was itself dropped in March, 1959.

Conceding defeat, the BBC tried another tack in its battle for the teen audiences and scheduled a new show, *Drumbeat*, to start at 6:30pm on April 4, 1959 – carefully scheduled so as not to compete with *Oh Boy!*, although the ITV show itself closed just a matter of a few weeks later.

The format was similar to that of *Oh Boy!* in that the screen was filled with as many dancers and musicians as possible and featured live, popular acts of the time. Among the many stars who appeared during the twenty two episodes which aired up until August 29, 1959 were the American Paul Anka and home grown Billy Fury, Cliff Richard, Dickie Valentine and Petula Clark.

The resident band was Bob Miller and The Millermen – rescued from the unsuccessful *Dig This!* and given a second chance, with support from The John Barry Seven, Vince Eager – brought over from *Oh Boy!* – and the newcomer Adam Faith, who would go on to register his first UK number 1 with "What Do You Want" in November, 1959.

Among the guests during the show were also The Lana Sisters, a trio who included in their number a certain Mary O'Brien – later to gain massive popularity as Dusty Springfield, firstly with her brother Tom in The Springfields and later in the early 1960's as a solo performer.

One other performer who successfully made the transition from the commercial television *Oh Boy!* to the BBC programme *Drumbeat* was the boogie-woogie piano playing singer Roy Young. Inspired by Bill Haley to concentrate on rock 'n' roll after spending much of his early years as a promising snooker player, Roy Young spent some time in London before gaining his first professional gig playing with Johnny Duncan and The Bluegrass Boys.

An audition for *Oh Boy!* followed in 1958, during which Roy played a Little Richard song so successfully that he was hired on the spot and given the nickname 'England's Little Richard.' He later became a regular performer on *Drumbeat* and the successor to *Oh Boy!*, *Boy Meets Girls* but despite several records released on the Fontana label, he failed to make a commercial impact on the charts.

When ITV closed *Oh Boy!* in May 1959, they replaced it with another Jack Good production, *Boy Meets Girls* – in this case the boy was Marty Wilde and the girls were the successful Vernons Girls. Good retained the organist Cherry Wainer – famous for her involvement with Lord Rockingham's X1 – and saxophonist Red Price, but although the show, which first went to air on Saturday, September 12, 1959, at first concentrated on up-beat songs, later episodes concentrated more on ballads as the rock 'n' roll bubble appeared to be bursting. The final episode aired on February 26, 1960

For their part, the BBC replaced *Drumbeat* by a new music orientated panel show named *Juke Box Jury*, during which the panellists –

a mixture of celebrities and audience members – would pass judgment on a number of newly released records. Hosted by the Radio Luxembourg disc jockey, David Jacobs – who had put forward a similar idea to the BBC some two years previously, but which was rejected at the time – the show proved to be extremely popular.

To add interest to the show, a performer of one of the records reviewed would be hidden from the panellists on what would become to be known as the "hot seat" and listen to the comments – and sometimes harsh criticism – from the panel members before being introduced to them.

The show was a great success and at its peak drew a viewing audience of over twelve million, but it also signalled the end of the TV rock 'n' roll shows of the first great British rock 'n' roll era.

The independent TV show *Wham!* – yet another Jack Good production – made a final attempt to draw in teenagers when it started in April, 1960 with stars such as Billy Fury, The Vernons Girls and Joe Brown, but lasted for just eight episodes before closing – the reason being that "the ABC thinks there is no longer a public for teenage rock 'n' roll programmes."

But of course it wasn't all down to television programmes – although the visual aspect of TV made these programmes more appealing – as radio, too, played a big part in gaining exposure for musical performers.

One of the first radio programmes to pick up on the skiffle boom was *Saturday Skiffle Club*, first broadcast on the BBC Light Programme on June 1, 1957. As the name suggests, it was aimed at the new "skiffle" craze sweeping the country and was originally broadcast for an hour at 10:00am each Saturday morning.

Early guests on the programme were obviously skiffle artists such as Chas McDevitt – who together with singer Nancy Whiskey had recorded the classic skiffle song "Freight Train" and taken it to number 5 in the UK charts – The Vipers Skiffle Group and Johnny

Duncan and His Bluegrass Boys. Lonnie Donegan, as the major skiffle star, was the obvious draw card and indeed made appearances on the show, but another aspiring performer, Cliff Richard, auditioned for the show but was not successful.

In October, 1958 the programme underwent several changes – its air time was increased to two hours, from 10:00am to midday, the name was changed to remove the word skiffle and a bigger budget enabled performers from the non-skiffle world to make appearances. The original presenter, Brian Matthew, was retained and his more relaxed manner on the new format set the style for a younger audience.

Restrictions on the amount of air time given to records meant that many performances were pre-recorded and broadcast as 'live' in preference to just playing a record. Restrictions imposed by the Musicians Union on overseas performers appearing in Britain enabled more home grown acts to appear, including the now more acceptable Cliff Richard, Adam Faith, Terry Dene, Vince Taylor and the guitarist Bert Weedon.

A relaxation of the Musicians Union brought more overseas performers to the programme as they attempted to gain publicity for their current tours – Eddie Cochran and Gene Vincent are typical cases – and after the flood gates opened performers of the calibre of Jerry Lee Lewis, Bo Diddley and The Everly Brothers also appeared. By August, 1959 the audience had reached five million listeners.

The list of UK artists who made the UK charts during the rock 'n' roll boom time is vast – many of them managed to hit the charts just the one time and returned to obscurity just a quickly as they had risen.

Who can remember, for example, Keith Kelly? An original member of The John Barry Seven, he left the group in 1959 and performed at the 2 I's coffee bar where he was noticed and signed by George Martin for Parlophone records. He made the top twenty with his first record, the self-penned "Tease Me", but his follow up "Listen Little Girl" made little impact.

A similar fate befell Nelson Keene, who so impressed Larry Parnes after hearing a demo tape sent to him that the impresario signed him and added Nelson to a summer show in Blackpool starring Joe Brown and Lance Fortune. Nelson Keene's first single "Image of a Girl" made the UK top forty but thereafter his career disintegrated.

Even Tommy Steele's brother, Colin Hicks, who was signed up by Larry Parnes in November, 1957, could not produce the same level of success as his more famous brother. Despite touring with Marty Wilde and making several records with the Pye label, Hicks and his band, The Cabin Boys, could not achieve chart success. His first single was "Empty Arms Blues" and featured, according to the record label "Mr. Parnes, Shillings and Pence".

After splitting from Hicks, two members of The Cabin Boys, keyboardist Mike O'Neill and bassist Rod 'Boots' Slade, together with guitarist Colin Green and drummer Laurie Jay, collaborated to form Nero and The Gladiators, who achieved chart success in March, 1961 with the rock 'n' roll version of the classic "Entry of the Gladiators".

A young singer who originally intended to make a career as a teacher, but who gained success with covers of American originals, Gary Miller is best remembered for his 1956 cover of the Dick James original theme song for the TV series *Robin Hood*, "Robin Hood" While the Dick James version reached number 14 in the UK charts, Gary Miller achieved his only top ten hit with his version in January, 1956.

Gary Miller also recorded other top twenty hits, both before and after "Robin Hood" – such as "The Yellow Rose Of Texas" in 1955, "The Garden Of Eden" (1957) and "The Story Of My Life" (1958) but the advent of rock 'n' roll effectively killed off his singing career.

He did achieve some success as the singing voice for the puppet character Troy Tempest in the popular TV series *Stingray* and had minor acting roles in programs such as *The Saint* and *Gideon's Way*, but Gary Miller was unable to achieve further chart success, with the exception of "There Goes That Song Again" , which peaked at number 29 in the UK charts in late 1961. Sadly Gary Miller died from a heart attack on June 15, 1968.

In the late 1950's it was almost unheard of for a British pop singer to have chart success in America, but, well before The Beatles conquered the world, another singer/songwriter from Liverpool achieved this distinction. What's more, while one side of his record was a hit in America, the flip side of the same record made the UK charts.

Figure 8 - Russ Hamilton
Photo courtesy of Barrie Smith

Ronald Hulme was born in Everton, Liverpool, and like many youngsters of the time started his career as a 'redcoat' at one of the popular Butlin's holiday camps after completing his national service.

Hulme formed a skiffle group with some of his musical fellow redcoats, which led to a recording contract with Oriole records. With a name change to become Russ Hamilton, his first record, "We Will Make Love" reached a peak of number 2 in the UK charts in May, 1957.

The record was also released in America where some confusion arose, which resulted in the flip side, "Rainbow" being plugged as the A side. This song proved extremely popular in America, selling over one million copies as it climbed to number 4 in the Billboard hot 100 charts.

The follow up record, also written by Hamilton and like his first hit in the UK supposedly inspired by his girlfriend of the time was called "Wedding Ring" but despite Hamilton's instant star status, only reached number 20 in the UK charts in September, 1957 and subsequent releases failed to chart at all.

By the end of the 1950's, Hamilton had faded totally from the UK music scene, and although he did obtain a recording contract with MGM records in Nashville he could never repeat the success of his one and only American hit.

Just as Russ Hamilton pre-dated The Beatles with his American success, another young singer was pre-dating The Bay City Rollers tartan stage gear.

The Scottish style was adopted by a young apprentice plumber from Leith, Edinburgh, Jackie Dennis. He was discovered by the English comedy duo Mike and Bernie Winters in 1958 and introduced to the agent Eve Taylor – one of the few female managers in the business and later to manage several pop acts, such as John Barry, Adam Faith and The Lana Sisters.

Jackie Dennis was booked on the *Six-Five Special* and made an immediate impact with his spiky hair, kilt and energetic stage act, even though he was just fifteen years old. His first record, a cover of the hit American record by Billie and Lillie "La Dee Dah" raced up the UK charts and reached number 4 in March, 1958. His second release, another cover – this time it was the quirky Sheb Wooley record "Purple People Eater" – peaked at number 29 at the end of June, 1958.

That was the final chart entry for Jackie Dennis, despite several appearances on television, including the *Perry Como* show in America and he faded almost as quickly as his meteoric rise.

Another youngster who had a transient impact on both the British and American charts was Laurie London. Born in Bethnal Green, London, Laurie was still attending The Davenant Foundation Grammar School and was just thirteen when he recorded an up-beat version of the spiritual song "He's Got The Whole World In His Hands" .

Accompanied by the Geoff Love Orchestra and released on the Parlophone record label, the record did moderately well in Britain when it peaked at number 12 in November, 1957. However, an association between the British Parlophone and Capitol records in America had the record released in America, where it reached number 2 on the Billboard record charts in April, 1958, remaining there for four weeks.

Although the record was Laurie London's only hit, the record was the most successful British male offering in America for the decade. London went on to record other songs in both English and German and was an entrant in the German Hit Festival in 1959 with the intriguingly named "Bum Ladda Bum Bum". Laurie London effectively retired from the music business – at just nineteen – and eventually became a hotel manager in West Sussex.

With artists achieving success from all over Britain, it is no surprise that Wales, with it's tradition and heritage of fine singing, should also produce a popular ballad singer in the 1950's – well before Tom Jones made his breakthrough.

Malcolm Vaughan started life as Malcolm James Thomas, in the coal mining villages of Abercynon and later Troedyrhiw in south

Wales. Although he had a fine voice as a youngster and was a member of the local choir, he set his sights on becoming an actor and by the time he had reached his mid-teens in 1944 he had performed on the stage in the West End production of the comedy play by Emlyn Williams entitled "The Druid's Rest".

Further West End performances followed, including a singing role in the musical comedy "Jenny Jones" and appearances in a variety show put together by the band leader Jack Hylton.

His acting career was put on hold in 1947 when he was called up for national service, during which he served in Egypt and Greece with the British Army. On his demobilization he returned to his stage career and eventually teamed up with the comedian Kenneth Earle, with whom he formed a double act.

Their proposed stage name of Earle and Thomas did not sound catchy enough, so Malcolm Thomas changed his surname to Vaughan – a change later made official by deed poll in 1963.

The duo performed in variety halls across the UK, with Vaughan providing the singing and straight man role to the comedian Earle. It was during one such performance, at the Chiswick Empire theatre in 1955 that the BBC radio presenter Jack Jackson was impressed by Vaughan's strong voice as he imitated the popular tenor of the time Mario Lanza.

Jackson arranged for Vaughan to audition for the HMV record producer Walter J Ridley, who was equally impressed and organized a recording contract for Vaughan. His first record, the strong ballad "Ev'ry Day Of My Life", reached number 5 in the UK charts in July, 1955.

Vaughan's next three releases failed to make significant progress in the UK charts, but his fifth release, "St. Therese Of The Roses" climbed to number 3 in the UK charts and proved to be one his biggest chart successes.

The record initially gained mixed reaction because of its religious content and the BBC even went so far as to ban it, stating that 'the lyric is contrary to both the Roman Catholic doctrine and to Protestant sentiment'. With the added publicity caused by the BBC ban, and with the record being played extensively on Radio Luxembourg, it raced up the charts to top out at number 3 in October, 1956.

Several more hits followed, including a top three position with "My Special Angel" in November, 1957 and "More Than Ever (Come Prima)" which reached number 5 in the UK charts in October, 1958, but by then the rock 'n' roll boom was well under way and Vaughan found it hard to compete and his recording career was all but over by 1960.

Just as with Malcolm Vaughan, there were several pop singers who achieved fame and fortune as a development of their acting careers. Two such singers come to mind in particular, Jess Conrad and John Leyton. Both started their singing careers as a direct result of their appearances in TV dramas, although their levels of success varied considerably.

London born Jess Conrad started life as Gerald Arthur James, although for obvious reasons he earned the nickname 'Jesse' James early in life after the American Wild West outlaw. He started his professional career as a film extra and repertory actor and in 1959, mainly as a result of his pop star looks, gained the starring role in the TV production of the play *Rock A Bye Barney* set around a rock 'n' roll character.

By this time Jesse James had become Jess Conrad and although his singing in the TV play was actually overdubbed by Garry Mills, his acting performance was good enough to gain him a part in the TV drama series *The Human Jungle*, set around a psychiatrist, played by the experienced actor Herbert Lom.

Jess Conrad's part in the second episode of the series, playing a reprise of his rock 'n' roll performance as Barney, but this time as the troubled young rock 'n' roller Danny Pace, called for him to perform four numbers as his character.

The producer Jack Good, of *Six-Five Special* fame, happened to watch the episode and considered Jess Conrad to be a candidate for his TV shows, and Conrad duly appeared in *Oh Boy!*, *Wham!* and *Boy Meets Girls*.

His reception by the female audiences was led to a recording contract with Decca records and his first single, "Cherry Pie" – a cover of the American duo Skip and Flip's hit – was released in 1960.

The record barely crept into the bottom end of the UK top forty, but this was considered sufficient to warrant further releases. His second offering, "Unless You Meant It" failed miserably and it seemed as if Conrad's short career as a pop singer was already over before it had begun.

However, his third release was more suited to his, shall we say, unpretentious singing voice and "Mystery Girl" moved into the charts, reaching a creditable number 18 in the UK charts in February, 1961.

Further releases failed to make any significant impact in the charts, but Jess Conrad did achieve the dubious distinction of having no less than seven of his records appearing in the Kenny Everett list of the World's Worst Records, with his top placing being the totally unforgettable "My Pullover" at number 6.

Sharing Jess Conrad's career start as an actor, John Leyton began his career under the auspices of the impresario Robert Stigwood, who in the late 1950's – having relocated from his native Australia – had begun to build up a small theatrical agency.

Through Stigwood's influence, John Leyton obtained a role in the TV series *Biggles* as the flying adventurer's companion Ginger. This small success did not however, lead to bigger and better roles, so Stigwood, banking on Leyton's good looks, arranged for him to attend a series of auditions with major recording companies, hoping for some success as a pop singer.

None of the major companies were interested in John Leyton as a singer, but the legendary independent producer, Joe Meek, was undeterred by Leyton's apparent lack of vocal talent and agreed to produce him in Meek's home studio in his flat above a leather goods shop in Holloway, London.

Meek's first production with John Leyton in 1960 was a cover version of the American Ray Patterson's tragic song "Tell Laura I Love Her" but Leyton's version was withdrawn by EMI, who had just taken over the record label Top Rank, to whom Meek and Stigwood had leased the recording, as another British act, Ricky Valance, had also released a version of the song through EMI. The Ricky Valance version went on to reach number 1 in the UK charts in September, 1960.

Leyton's second Meek produced song "The Girl On The Floor Above" although released on the HMV label, also failed to trouble the chart compilers.

In mid-1961, when it appeared that John Leyton's singing career would follow that of his predecessor Jess Conrad, when in an uncanny coincidence Leyton was offered the role of a pop singer in a TV production – this time the nationally broadcast TV series *Harpers West One*.

Stigwood again used his influence to arrange that Leyton's character, Johnny St. Cyr, would perform a song during the show and called upon Meek's song writing partner, Geoff Goddard, to come up with a suitable composition.

The result was John Leyton's number 1 hit, "Johnny, Remember Me" in August, 1961 and, boosted by further broadcasts during the TV series, went on to stay in the UK charts for fifteen weeks. His follow up single, "Wild Wind" peaked at number 2 in the UK charts in October, 1961 and set the stage for the Joe Meek/Robert Stigwood style of independent music production which would shape the industry for the next few years.

Although John Leyton failed to repeat the success of his first two hits, he released a series of Meek produced records over the next year, with the final Meek production being "Down The River Nile" in July, 1962, which barely crept into the top fifty charts. After this, Robert Stigwood took over the role of producer, perhaps increasing the quality of the recording, but somehow lacking in that 'Joe Meek Sound'.

As Leyton's pop career nose-dived, his acting career began to take off and during the 1960's appeared in several top rate movies, including *The Great Escape*, *Guns At Batasi* and the 1965 film *Von Ryan's Express* – in which he appeared alongside Frank Sinatra and Trevor Howard.

However, despite the – albeit temporary – success of actors Jess Conrad and John Leyton, the more normal route to fame and fortune was through the skiffle craze.

But out of the thousands of teenagers who were inspired by the skiffle craze and set their sights on a musical career, only a few would achieve success. What is more unusual is for the same performer to achieve success twice under different names and under different pseudonyms.

The story of how a young roadie could have not one but two careers in pop music over two decades is unusual, to say the least.

Bernard William Jewry was born in Muswell Hill in London during the Second World War, but moved to Mansfield, Nottinghamshire while still a young boy, where he developed an interest in pop music. Although unable to gain status as a performer, he spent his time as a roadie for a young band calling themselves Johnny Theakstone and The Tremolos

The band, in the hope of gaining fame and fortune, had recorded a demo tape and sent it to the BBC to see if they could be offered a spot on the radio programme *Saturday Club*. While waiting for a response, the group's singer, John Theakstone, had decided that the group needed a more commercial name and came up with the name Shane Fenton and The Fentones.

Before the BBC could respond to the demo tape, John Theakstone tragically died as the result of rheumatic fever he had suffered as a child. The group was naturally devastated and decided to break up, but before this happened the BBC had responded and invited them to come to London for an audition.

Figure 9 - Shane Fenton
Shane Fenton, later to find fame a decade later as Alvin Stardust, seen here
with composer Lionel Bart in 1962
© Victoria and Albert Museum, London

John Theakstone's mother persuaded the group to stay together and retain the group name to honour her son, but to be able to perform at the audition they obviously need a new singer. Searching for a replacement, the members of the group decided to give their young roadie a try out.

Bernard Jewry was successful and duly took the stage name Shane Fenton – which he later took permanently by deed poll – before the group headed for London and their audition.

The group passed the audition with flying colours and within a week had landed a recording contract with EMI. The group's first single, "I'm A Moody Guy" was released in September, 1961 on the Parlophone label and reached number 22 in the UK charts, thanks largely to an appearance on the TV show *Thank Your Lucky Stars*.

The group was signed up by Larry Parnes and toured the UK in one of Parnes' package tours, joining Billy Fury and The Tornados, Peter Jay and The Jaywalkers and The Karl Denver Trio.

However further releases by the group, including an instrumental by The Fentones called "Lover's Guitar", failed to have any impact, despite the group being well-received as a live band, until the single "Cindy's Birthday" once again returned them to the charts, peaking at number 19 in 1962.

The roller coaster ride continued, with further releases failing to hit the charts and despite appearing in yet another Parnes' package tour – this time as bottom of the bill – the group decided to call it quits and broke up, leaving Shane Fenton to continue as a solo act.

This may have been the end of the story for many and indeed Shane Fenton, although performing under the name of Shane Fenton and Iris – the latter being his wife Iris Caldwell, the sister of the singer Rory Storm - in clubs in the north of England, was not destined to find more performing success under that name.

Fenton also tried his hand at show business management, teaming up with his own manager, Tommy Sanderson, to manage the group The Hollies – who included Bobby Elliot, ex-drummer in the Fentones in their line up and who were about to reach greater heights than Shane Fenton could ever dream of.

However, after a decade the musical fashion in Britain had undergone many, many changes and, following on from Mersey Beat in the 1960's, the early 1970's saw the rise of a new phenomenon – glam rock.

With a new manager, Hal Carter, and a new record deal with Magnet records, the 1960's Shane Fenton was reborn as the leather-clad glam rocker Alvin Stardust. Under this new persona, Alvin Stardust made several entries into the UK carts, with his debut single "My Coo Ca Choo" reaching number 2 and the follow up "Jealous Mind" finally giving him a number 1 record in 1973 – a decade after his first chart success with The Fentones.

By the end of 1960, the British pop music scene had quietened down somewhat from the heady days of 1958 and 1959. The early rock 'n roll pioneers had moved on to become all-round entertainers and a glance through the chart listings of late 1960 shows a remarkable absence of rock 'n' roll records, even from the American acts who had started it all just a couple of years ago.

Little Richard had announced his retirement from rock music in late 1957 while touring Australia, claiming that he had been told by God to give up rock 'n' roll. Elvis Presley had been drafted into the army in March, 1958 and Jerry Lee Lewis had been sent home from his UK tour in May the same year when it was revealed that he had married his thirteen year old first cousin, Myra Brown.

Buddy Holly, The Big Bopper and Ritchie Valens had all died in that tragic plane crash in Iowa in 1959 – the day the music died, according to Don McLean. Eddie Cochran was also dead, killed in a traffic accident near Bath in April 1960, the same accident which seriously injured Gene Vincent.

Bill Haley was considered too old by the teenagers and The Everly Brothers had forsaken the raw sounds of "Wake Up Little Susie" and "Bye Bye Love" for the sweeter sounds of "When Will I Be Loved."

Of the new acts coming from America, the majority seemed to have forsaken rock 'n' roll for the more middle of the road sound, with the notable exceptions of Johnny and The Hurricanes – "Beatnik Fly" and "Red River Rock" – Duane Eddy – "Shazam" – and Freddy Cannon – "Way Down Yonder In New Orleans."

The British pioneers of rock 'n' roll had also forsaken their early rawness for a more polished style. Artists such as Cliff Richard, Billy Fury and Tommy Steele had made the transition to film performers while other early rockers such as Marty Wilde and Joe Brown had toned down their acts.

But there were a few performers determined to break away from the all too pervasive comfortable styles as demonstrated by the likes of Craig Douglas, Anthony Newley and even the comedian Ken Dodd.

You would be hard pressed to find a stronger contrast to this blend of smoothness and professionalism than David Sutch. Better known under his stage name of Screaming Lord Sutch, he brought a theatrical stage presence to his performance that was not reflected in his record sales.

David Edward Sutch was born in Hampstead, London in November, 1940 – in the midst of the London blitz. Although not connected in any way to the British peerage, Sutch adopted the stage name of Screaming Lord Sutch, the third Earl of Harrow, after being inspired by the American performer Screamin' Jay Hawkins, who had scored big with his shock-rock performance of "I Put A Spell On You" in 1956.

Sutch's first record, released in late 1961 on the HMV record label, was "Til The Following Night", backed by a cover of the rock 'n' roll classic "Good Golly Miss Molly", and was produced by Joe Meek. Despite the best efforts of the legendary producer, the record, attributed to Screaming Lord Sutch and The Savages, failed to reach the charts.

Further releases were slow to follow, as the band concentrated more on their live performances, which were based on horror themes, including an opening sequence in which Sutch appeared rising from a coffin – and this was long before Alice Cooper.

A highlight of the stage show was the song "Jack The Ripper" and this became the group's second single in March, 1963, again produced by Joe Meek but this time on the Decca record label. Once again it failed to reach the charts and a third single, reportedly a spoof on the popular Mark Wynter song "Venus In Blue Jeans" entitled "Monster In Black Tights" also failed.

Undeterred, Screaming Lord Sutch and The Savages continued to release records produced by Joe Meek, but chart success eluded them.

The band has numerous personnel changes during their career, with later well-known musicians such as pianists Nicky Hopkins and Freddie 'Fingers' Lee, guitarist Ritchie Blackmore and drummer Carlo Little all appearing in the line-up in the early 1960's. Later members included Noel Redding and Mitch Mitchell from The Jimi Hendrix Experience, Mick Abrahams, original guitarist with Jethro Tull and Clem Cattini from Johnny Kidd and The Pirates and later The Tornados.

David Sutch also tried his hand at politics, beginning in 1963 when he stood as the National Teenage Party candidate at the Stratford-upon-Avon by election caused by the resignation of John Profumo during the political scandal of the time. Sutch received just 208 votes and set the trend for his later political career – which included his founding of the Official Monster Raving Loony Party in 1983 – when he managed to contest and lose 40 different elections.

Another unlikely and welcome change from the blandness was a gravel voiced porter working at London's Covent Garden fruit and vegetable market named Thomas Charles Bruce. His neighbour, Barry Mason, happened to be in the music business as a songwriter, heard the unusual voice and suggested that Tommy, as the porter liked to be called, make a recording.

The song chosen was the Fats Waller favourite "Ain't Misbehavin'" and Tommy Bruce sang it in the style of The Big Bopper with, as he himself put it, his "sandpaper and gravel voice sounding diabolical" complete with a strong East London accent – Tommy was from Stepney, after all.

The freshness and naturalness of the recording resonated with the record buying public and the now ex-porter enjoyed his first chart success with a number 3 position. His next record, "Broken Doll" however was less successful and barely climbed into the top forty. However, the popularity he gained from his one and only top ten record was sufficient to gain him many concert and TV appearances.

Another singer with a distinct voice to break through in the early 1960's and with a similar background to Cliff Richard, in that he was born in India, was Richard Graham Sarstedt.

The Sarstedt family – his mother, two brothers Peter[7] and Clive and three sisters moved to England following the death of his father in 1954 and it was while still attending Heath Clark Grammar School in Croydon that the Sarstedt boys formed a skiffle group named The Fabulous Five.

Winning a talent contest at the Classic Cinema in Chelsea gained young Richard the contract to record an advertising jingle for the Cadbury's drinking chocolate firm, to be played on Radio Luxembourg.

His management team of Michael Barclay and Philip Waddilove decided that Richard Sarstedt was not the most catchy name for a pop singer and, after seeing the success achieved by Adam Faith, decided on another name with biblical connotations, Eden, and then, searching for a surname, decided on Kane, after the film *Citizen Kane* a particular favourite of Michael Barclay at the time.

The advertising jingle – named "Hot Chocolate Crazy" – was released as a single on the Pye label in August, 1960, but failed to chart. Switching to Decca, Eden Kane was given the Les Vandyke song "Well I Ask You" as his first single for the new label and in August, 1961 the song reached number 1 in the UK charts.

Three more top ten chart hits followed in close succession – "Get Lost", "Forget Me Not" and "I Don't Know Why" – and Eden Kane was on the road to success, joining tours by Billy Fury and Cliff Richard. Chart success proved more elusive, however, and it was not until 1964 that he managed a further chart entry, with "Boys Cry" in January, 1964, but this to be his final hit.

While the fellow Indian born Cliff Richard appeared to have turned his back on rock 'n' roll by 1960, favouring songs such as "Voice in the Wilderness" and "I Love You", his backing group, originally called The Drifters but now known as The Shadows since early 1959 began to make a name for themselves in their own right.

The group's first two singles – as The Drifters – and their third, as The Shadows, gained very little success, despite Cliff Richard's popularity. However things changed dramatically for the group in 1960, when the Jerry Lordan composition "Apache" reached number 1 in the UK charts in July, despite competition from the already well known guitarist Bert Weedon, whose version only managed to reach number 24.

The single set the style for instrumental groups for the future, with the combination of three guitars and drums proving a blue print for others to follow. The cutting sound of the lead guitar contrasting with the driving rhythm guitar and backed by the tight bass and drums combination proved a winning formula and future Shadows releases would follow the same pattern closely.

The successful line up of Hank B. Marvin (lead guitar), Bruce Welch (rhythm guitar), 'Jet' Harris (bass guitar) and Tony Meehan (drums) continued to have chart success with their next releases, including classics such as "Man Of Mystery", "F.B.I.", "The Frightened City" and "Kon Tiki" before Tony Meehan left the group in October, 1961, to be replaced by Brian Bennett. Shortly after, in April, 1962, Brian 'Liquorice' Locking replaced Jet Harris.

The Shadows, under various line-ups continued to be successful chart performers throughout the 1960's, with original members Hank Marvin and Bruce Welch celebrating fifty years in the limelight with a 50th Anniversary tour beginning in 2009 which took them through Europe and on to Australia, New Zealand and South Africa.

But while Tommy Bruce, Eden Kane and The Shadows scored chart success with styles that stood out from the rest, it was another group that would provide what was to be perhaps the last hurrah for rock 'n' roll in the early days of the 1960's, as well as setting the scene for future theatrical stage performers such as Alice Cooper and coming up with a musical line up that would influence great artists in the future such as Led Zeppelin and The Who.

Like many contemporaries, the story of Johnny Kidd and The Pirates begins in the skiffle years. Born in Willesden, London in December, 1939, Frederick Heath formed a skiffle group – originally called Bats Heath and The Vampires, which soon became The Five Nutters and then The Fred Heath Band – with close friend Alan Caddy. As rock 'n' roll began to eclipse skiffle, Heath and Caddy joined with Tony Docherty, Johnny Gordon and Ken McKay to form a more rock orientated group.

By 1959 the group had come to the attention of the well known producer Walter J Ridley – who had already achieved great success with Alma Cogan, Malcolm Vaughan, Max Bygraves and a host of other popular singers in the early 1950's – who signed the group to the HMV label, part of the massive EMI group which included Cliff Richard's Columbia label.

It was during the recording of the group's first single, "Please Don't Touch" in April, 1959 that a sound engineer reputedly came up with the name Johnny Kidd and The Pirates and the name stuck.

The first single achieved moderate success, reaching number 25 in the UK charts in June, 1959 but the follow up, "Feelin'" failed to make any impression in the charts.

The next single was cover of the song "You've Got What It Takes" and indeed the group did have what it takes, as the song again reached number 25 in the UK charts and would possibly have achieved greater success, but for the competition from Marv Johnson, whose version reached number 5.

There was a change in the Pirates line up before the next single was recorded. Brian Gregg took over on bass from Johnny Gordon while the drumming was handled by Clem Cattini. In the studio the lead guitar for their next record was the responsibility of session man Joe Moretti, who produced the spine tingling intro to "Shakin' All Over".

The song proved to be the group's biggest ever hit record, peaking at number 1 in August, 1960.

The group continued to develop their stage act following the success of the single and can be considered the pre-cursors of theatrical rock 'n' roll, pre-dating acts such as Alice Cooper by several years. With Johnny Kidd sporting an eye patch, wearing pirate's clothes and brandishing a cutlass and The Pirates also in full pirate regalia, the effect on audiences was one of amazement.

The unusual line up – for the time – of a single guitar, bass and drums also left a deep impression on future bands. According to the liner notes on The Who's *Live At Leeds* LP from 1970, which includes their version of "Shakin' All Over", the song is the best ever pre-Beatles rock 'n' roll song. It is also rumoured that The Who's singer, Roger Daltrey, gave up playing a guitar onstage so that The Who line up would more closely replicate that of The Pirates.

The group could not repeat the success of their number 1 single, however and further releases only dented the lower portions of the UK charts. Clem Cattini and Alan Caddy both left the Pirates and were soon joined by Brian Gregg as the trio headed off to join The Tornados, who were soon to have a number 1 hit on their hands with "Telstar", produced by the legendary Joe Meek.

A rebuilt Pirates – consisting of Cuddly Dudley's backing group, The Redcaps, Johnny Spence (bass), Johnny Patto (Guitar) and Frank Farley (drums) – were in rehearsal when Johnny Patto left, to be re-placed by Mick Green, also from The Redcaps.

The new formation recorded a cover version of Arthur Alexander's "(Just) A Shot Of Rhythm And Blues" – later famously covered by The Beatles – which reached number 48 in the UK charts at the end of 1962, and which is considered by many as the first cross-over between British rock 'n' roll and R & B music.

By then Mersey beat was reaching out to conquer the world, so as a compromise Johnny Kidd And The Pirates released their 'Beat Boom' single "I'll Never Get Over You" which went on to reach number 4 in the UK charts in July, 1963.

But from then on the charts would echo to the sounds of The Beatles, Gerry and The Pacemakers, The Swinging Blue Jeans, The Hollies, The Searchers, The Big Three, The Merseybeats, The Rolling Stones and countless others as the second great British musical happening exploded....

Chapter Five – Where are the Girls?

"It is all sha-la-la-la la la la lah"
(Al Stewart – Class of '58)

At first glance it seems that the UK charts in the mid to late 1950's were dominated by male singers – either the more mature balladeers and crooners before 1956, whose audience was mainly adults, or the younger, exciting rock 'n' roll artists that appealed to the teenage audiences.

Certainly it is true that female performers found it difficult to achieve chart success in the male dominated music business, and there were very few indeed who made it to the top in the raunchier world of rock 'n' roll.

As rock 'n' roll swept across America, the story was much the same, with male performers dominating the rock scene. However, there were some exceptions, in the shape of artists such as Wanda Jackson and Brenda Lee.

In the early days of her career Wanda Jackson would often appear on the same bill as Elvis Presley, who encouraged her rock 'n' roll efforts. In 1958 she listed in the UK charts at number 40 with the song "Mean, Mean Man" and in 1960 with "Let's Have a Party". Her recording of "Honey Bop" also caused some interest in the UK but failed to make the charts.

Brenda Lee scored American chart success in 1957 with the song "Dynamite", which earned her the nickname 'Little Miss Dynamite' in a reference to her height – she was just 4' 9" tall – and her powerful voice. She charted in the UK in 1959 with up beat records such as "Let's Jump the Broomstick" and "Sweet Nothin's", but her final UK chart listing for that year was the ballad "I'm Sorry".

But in the main female singers were more refined, and the UK charts of the mid to late 1950's featured American female singers in the style of the wholesome Doris Day or the more pop orientated Connie Francis, who scored UK chart success with "Who's Sorry Now" and "Stupid Cupid".

But what of the British female performers? Apart from a couple of records by the little known Janice Peters in 1958 ("This Little Girl's Goin' Rockin'" – a cover of the Ruth Brown American recording) and again in 1959 (the Ian Samwell written "A Girl Likes"), both in the Brenda Lee/Wanda Jackson rockabilly style, there was little to shout about on the female rock 'n' roll front.

Although she didn't make the charts as a soloist, the Hammond organ playing Cherry Wainer did have a number 1 UK chart hit as part of the infamous Lord Rockingham's XI in "Hoots Mon" in 1958.

Apart from these two, rock 'n' roll successes for British female acts were limited, to say the least. However, several British female performers did have chart successes in the late 1950's, albeit in a less exuberant style.

While America had The Andrews Sisters, highly successful during the war years entertaining the allied troops in their home country as well as Europe, Britain's equivalent during the 1950's were The Beverley Sisters.

The three sisters, Joy and the twins Teddie and Babs had a string of hit records, starting with "I Saw Mommy Kissing Santa Claus" in 1953 and even at the height of the rock 'n' roll era managed to chart with "The Little Drummer Boy" in 1959. But rock 'n' roll they were definitely not.

The Liverpool based football pools company, Vernons, had a range of social activities for their staff, including the formation of a staff choir. Starting off as a purely amateur group, the choir performed old favourites at old people's homes and similar venues on a charitable basis.

However, the high standard of their performances gave food for thought to the company and the group was soon working on a more professional basis as a publicity venture for the firm.

Originally the choir was made up from female workers at the company who were employed to check the pools coupons, but as the demand for professional engagements grew, the company began to import professional singers from outside the company.

Despite their obviously advertising name, The Vernons Girls were recruited by Jack Good as regulars for his first TV show, the *Six-Five Special*. The BBC had a strict policy banning advertising, so it is unclear how the group managed to retain a name that was obviously a promotion for the pools company.

The troupe, at this stage consisting of sixteen singers and dancers with a couple of backups, were a great success on the show, providing a good counterpoint to the otherwise male domination and Jack Good took them with him to his succeeding shows on independent television, *Oh Boy!* and *Boy Meets Girls* where The Vernons Girls played the girls to Marty Wilde's boy.

The group made several records under their own name and also provided backing vocals on many other records of the time, but it was not until 1962 that they achieved chart success with "Lover Please" which peaked at number 16 in May and a version of "Locomotion" which reached number 47 of that year.

The group disbanded shortly after, although several members retained an interest in the music business, with Vickie Haseman[8] marrying Joe Brown and Joyce Baker marrying Marty Wilde, both marriages producing successful offspring in Sam and Pete Brown and Kim and Ricky Wilde respectively.

But what of the solo female performers?

The main paths to exposure and stardom for many of the top British female names of the early to mid 1950's where through BBC radio and TV, dance halls, hotels and working men's clubs across the country. One such performer who gained her breakthrough in the early 1950's through television was the Irish born Ruby Murray.

Ruby Florence Murray was a child prodigy and after a throat operation as a young child, which gave her a unique sweet, yet husky tone, she was in demand in the area around her home town of Belfast. She performed on Irish TV at the age of twelve and, with her mother acting as chaperone, toured both Ireland and Scotland in variety shows.

It was while performing in the touring show "Yankee Doodle Blarney" in London's Metropolitan Music Hall in 1954 that she was spotted by Richard Afton, a TV producer who coincidentally had been responsible for Ruby's Irish TV performance. He was looking for a replacement resident singer for his BBC TV show *Quite Contrary* to replace Joan Regan, another popular singer of the day.

The record producer Ray Martin from Columbia records was impressed by Ruby's very first appearance on the show and as a result she was signed to Columbia records at just 19 years of age.

Her first single, "Heartbeat" was released as a 78rpm but despite this reached number 3 in the UK charts in December, 1954 and her second release, "Softly, Softly" became her first chart topper, reaching number 1 in January, 1955.

Ruby Murray could do no wrong in 1955, and became the first popular music performer – male or female – to have five records listed in the top twenty at the same time during March, 1955. That feat has to date only been equalled by Elvis Presley and Madonna.

By the end of the 1950's however, Ruby Murray's chart career was over, although she remained well-loved and popular through the 1960's and 1970's. She died on December 18, 1996.

A contemporary of Ruby Murray, and one of the few female performers to be a consistent top performer during the 1950's and early 1960's was Alma Cogan.

Alma Cogan was born in Whitechapel, in the eastern suburbs of London, in May, 1932. Christened Alma Angela Cohen, she was encouraged in her show business aspirations by her mother, who, when Alma was just eleven years old, entered her in the Sussex Queen of Song contest held at the popular sea-side resort of Brighton on the south coast.

Despite her youth, Alma managed to win a prize in the contest and went on to gain acclaim from the popular war time songstress Vera Lynn, who encouraged the young singer to participate in a variety show held in the Grand Theatre in Brighton.

At just sixteen years of age, Alma auditioned for the band leader Ted Heath, then one of the biggest names on the British big band scene. Heath was impressed, but thought that Alma was too young and advised her to come back again in five years time. He was later reputed to say that "letting her go was the biggest mistake of my life"

Undismayed by the rejection – although buoyed by the praise – Alma shared her musical interests with attending Worthing Art College, where she studied dress design – developing a skill that would help her stand out in her later career. In her spare time she could be found singing at local tea dances – a peculiarly British tradition.

To avoid the expenses of holding an evening dinner, socialites would often prefer to hold what would these days be the equivalent to a garden party. The tradition goes back to the 1880's and was popular more in the suburbs than in the city. The name comes from the types of refreshments served – coffee, fruit, sandwiches, occasionally champagne or claret but mainly tea – and an integral part of the proceedings was a small orchestra to provide entertainment for the guests.

Building on her growing reputation as a singer at these functions, in 1948 Alma gained small roles in the musical *High Button Shoes* and a revue titled *Sauce Tartare* in which she was joined by a young Audrey Hepburn.

Her big break, however, came when she was spotted by Walter J. Ridley, an executive at HMV records while singing for the evening diners at the Cumberland Hotel, who arranged a recording contract for the then still teenaged Alma.

The 45-rpm vinyl single was still some years away, so Alma's first record "To Be Worthy of You" was released in 1952 as a 78-rpm, as were many of her early single releases. In 1954 she recorded and released a cover version of the American hit "Bell Bottom Blues" originally released by Teresa Brewer and this proved to be Alma's first chart success, reaching number 4 in the UK charts in April that year.

Other chart successes followed, helped by her appearances on the BBC popular comedy radio show *Take It From Here*. Her first number 1 hit was "Dreamboat" which topped the UK charts for three weeks in July, 1955 and all told she managed to appear in the UK charts no less than eighteen times during the 1950's.

Alma Cogan was without doubt the foremost female British singer of the latter half of the 1950's, being judged the "Outstanding British Female Singer" by the music paper New Musical Express (NME) four times between 1956 and 1960.

Although billed as "the girl with a giggle in her voice" and well known for her extravagant stage dresses – reputedly designed by herself - she was capable of singing all types of material and did record at least one rock 'n' roll song, "Pink Shoelaces", in 1959 – which failed to make the charts – and made several appearances on *Oh Boy!* She was also a member of the jury on the TV programme *Juke Box Jury* for its first broadcast on June 1, 1959.

Alma Cogan moved into the 1960's by attempting to update her style to suit the new mood of the country, recording an impressive version of The Exciters song "Tell Him", but it was the Billie Davis version which proved to be successful in the UK in 1963. Alma also recorded "Tennessee Waltz" as a rock 'n' roll ballad in 1964, but although this release held the number 1 spot in Sweden for five weeks and also charted in Denmark, it failed to register in the UK.

Alma Cogan's life and career was cut short in 1966, when she sadly died of cancer following a collapse while touring Sweden in September. She died in Middlesex Hospital from ovarian cancer on October 26, 1966 at the age of just 34.

A contemporary of Alma Cogan, but an artist who went on to achieve greater success in the 1960's and 1970's was Petula Clark.

Like Alma Cogan, Petula Clark made her first singing appearance in 1939 when she sang with an orchestra on the steps leading in to Bentall's Department Store in Kingston upon Thames. As a reward, the seven year old Petula was given a tin of toffees and a gold wristwatch.

Born in 1932, Petula Sally Olwen Clark had ambitions as a young child to be an actress, but from her earliest beginnings it seemed that the path to stardom was to come from singing. Apart from her appearance mentioned above, Petula gained her first radio exposure just two years later.

Her father had taken her to a BBC radio broadcast aimed at British troops serving overseas. It was October, 1942, with bombing raids over London a nightly occurrence and the broadcast was halted temporarily because of an air raid warning.

The producer, attempting to calm down a nervous and fidgety audience, called for a volunteer to sing from the audience. Petula duly obliged with a rendition of the 1901 Stanton and Nevin 'dialect' song "Mighty Lak' a Rose".

The producer, impressed by the overwhelming response from the studio audience, persuaded Petula to repeat the performance during the resumed broadcast to the troops resulting in more than 500 appearances in similar broadcasts over the remainder of the war.

She became known as the "Singing Sweetheart" and was adopted as a good luck mascot by British troops, with her photo carried into battle stuck on the side of many a British tank.

In 1944 she realized her childhood ambition to act when she was spotted by the film producer Maurice Elvy while performing at the Royal Albert Hall and subsequently given roles in several British films, working alongside established film stars of the time such as Anthony Newley and Alec Guinness.

But it was as a singer that she was to achieve her greatest successes. In 1954 she released her first hit record "The Little Shoemaker" on the Polygon record label – part owned by her father – and went on to score in 1955 with "Majorca" and "Suddenly There's a Valley".

By 1960, Petula Clark had focused her career in France, signing for the Vogue record label, and her UK career was on the wane. However, her recording of "Downtown" in 1964 was the vehicle for a major comeback as the record went to number 1 across the world, including the UK, Australia and America.

"Downtown" was awarded the Grammy for the "Best Rock & Roll Recording of 1964" and was the trigger for a series of 15 consecutive chart entries in America, including "I Know a Place" and "I Couldn't Live Without Your Love".

Petula Clark continued making records and films and appearing in stage shows right up to the current date, proving that the young singer once dubbed as England's Shirley Temple had what it takes to become a highly successful all round entertainer.

But not all successful British female entertainers in the 1950's and early 1960's were vocalists. The piano had long played an important role in popular music, right from Scott Joplin's ragtime, with the syncopation of the right hand bouncing along to a heavy octave-chord rhythm of the left, through the jazz greats like Art Tatum and Thelonious Monk and the swing of Nat 'King' Cole.

But as far as British pianists are concerned, the first to bring piano playing to the pop audiences was the Trinidad born Winifred Atwell.

Winifred studied the piano as a child in Trinidad and gained a good reputation playing locally for American servicemen at the nearby Piarco air force base. It was there she gained her first experience of the boogie-woogie style of playing, when one airman bet her that she couldn't play in that style.

The next day Winifred returned, having composed a boogie-woogie piece that she called "Piarco Rag" – although this was later renamed as "Five Finger Boogie" – to win the bet.

Although she had trained as a pharmacist in the expectation that she would follow in the family business, the piano was her real love and Winifred soon left for America to continue her love affair and study with Alexander Borovsky, the Russian born pianist and winner of the 1912 Anton Rubenstein competition.

Shortly after the end of the war Winifred moved to London and gained a place at the Royal Academy of Music, where she went on to be awarded the Academy's highest grading for musicianship – the first female pianist to achieve that honour.

To support her studies, Winifred played in small clubs and theatres in the evenings, learning more and more of the popular rag time techniques and honing her stagecraft.

It was during one of these appearances, at the Casino Theater while standing in for a sick fellow musician, that she caught the eye of the Russian-born entrepreneur Bernard Delfont and was signed by Decca records.

Despite popular acclaim, initially her records failed to reach the charts and it was not until she released "Britannia Rag" that she achieved chart success in December. 1952, when the tune reached number 11. This was quickly followed by "Coronation Rag" in May, 1953, "Flirtation Waltz" in September of the same year and "Let's Have a Party" in December, 1953.

Her success continued in 1954 mainly through her honky-tonk piano sound, although she interspersed this with a classical-inspired recording of "Rachmaninoff's 18th Variation on a Theme by Paganini" – thankfully for the record buying public sub-titled "The Story of Three Loves" which reached number 9 in the UK charts in July, 1954.

Her first number 1 was the honky-tonk "Let's Have Another Party" in December, 1954 – the first piano instrumental record to reach number 1 – and she continued to chart over the next few years, her popularity boosted by sell-out concerts and her own TV series on the newly formed ITV network in 1956.

Her unique piano sound was attributed to what became known as her 'other piano' – a beat up upright piano bought by her husband, the former comedian Lew Levisohn, for just 50 shillings from a junk shop in Battersea.

Winifred would normally start her concert appearances playing a classical grand piano, before switching to the battered honky-tonk, always introducing it as her other piano. This piano became famous in its own write and her records were often attributed to 'Winifred Atwell and her other piano'.

Winifred Atwell is probably best remembered by the British public for her tune "Black and White Rag", which the BBC has used as the signature tune for the popular TV snooker programme *Pot Black* for several decades.

The success of Winifred Atwell in the mid 1950's increased the popularity and acceptance of the piano in popular music and paved the way for other pianists in the same genre, notably Russ Conway, who had several records in the UK charts at the end of the 1950's, including the number 1 hits "Side Saddle" and "Roulette".

Another pianist to gain popularity as a result of Winifred Atwell's success was Gladys Mills, more popularly known as Mrs. Mills, who continued the Atwell style of honky-tonk music with a string of releases in the early 1960's, most of which contained the word 'Party' in the title.

But back to the vocalists. Arguably one of the finest of British female performers during the second half of the last century was Shirley Bassey, who first achieved fame in the late 1950's with the unlikely hit "The Banana Boat Song".

Shirley Veronica Bassey was born and raised in the tough district of Tiger Bay, Cardiff, in Wales. Her powerful voice was noted while at school although, according to Shirley, her music teacher advised her to back off, until she was singing out in the corridor.

She left school at the early age of 14 and while working during the daytime in the packing department of a local factory, she could be found in the evenings singing in the local pubs and clubs. By 1953 she had signed up for her first real professional job, touring with the variety show *Memories of Jolson*, based on the life of the legendary Al Jolson.

A further stint in the show *Hot from Harlem* followed but when this show closed and she fell pregnant – at just 16 – she became disillusioned and withdrew from show business to work as a waitress in Cardiff.

What could have been a very short career was resuscitated when a local booking agent, Michael Sullivan, seeing the talent in Shirley despite her young age, booked her in at shows in local theatres. It was here that she was spotted by the entrepreneur Jack Hylton, who persuaded her to appear in his West End show *Such Is Life*, starring the highly popular radio comedian Al Read, in the Adelphi Theater.

During the show's run, Shirley was noticed by Johnny Franz, the A&R manager at Philips records. Her first record for Philips was "Burn My Candle", released in 1956, with lyrics so suggestive that it was banned by the BBC – a not unusual occurrence in those days owing to the strict code of conduct that the BBC enforced.

Further releases followed, all selling reasonably well despite not impacting the charts, until her breakthrough came in February, 1957 when "The Banana Boat Song" – a cover of the Harry Belafonte recording – reached number 8 in the UK charts. Considering that the Belafonte version had reached number 2, this was a most impressive chart debut.

Her next release was "Fire Down Below" which reached number 30 in August, 1957 but her next release "Puh Leeze Mister Brown" failed to make any impact. It seemed as if her career was once again on the wane, as her next release, recorded in the middle of 1958, the ballad "Hands Across The Sea" backed by "As I Love You" was a slow seller.

A chance performance at the London Palladium changed matters around, however, and it was the B side which began to climb the charts. In January, 1959, "As I Love You" became Shirley Bassey's first number 1 hit and the first number 1 by a Welsh artist.

While "As I Love You" began slowly to climb the charts, Shirley had again been busy in the studios recording "Kiss Me, Honey Honey, Kiss Me". When this was released it too entered the charts and reached number 3 the same time that "As I Love You" was at number 1.

A switch of record labels to EMI's Columbia followed shortly after and it was under this label that she recorded and released "As Long As He Needs Me" from the stage show *Oliver!*, written by Lionel Bart. This record reached number 2 on the UK charts in August, 1960 and Shirley Bassey went on to record many more hit records over the coming decades, including the title song from the hugely successful James Bond film *Goldfinger*.

Apart from the song "Sailor", recorded and charted by both Petula Clark – whose version reached number 1 in January, 1961 – and the wartime favourite Anne Shelton – whose version was number 10 the same week as the Petula Clark version – the next British female vocalist to reach the top ten in the UK charts was the teenage sensation Helen Shapiro.

Even from an early age, Helen Kate Shapiro had decided that she wanted to become a jazz singer and her role models were artists such as Judy Garland and Frank Sinatra, certainly unusual for a pre-teenager.

Her first venture into show business was as a member of the group Susie and The Hula Hoops, a group formed at her school and which included her cousin, Susan Singer, and a young Mark Field – both of whom were successful in the 1960's, the latter being more well known under his stage name Marc Bolan.

Guided more by the success than the style of Alma Cogan, Helen studied singing at the Maurice Burman School of Pop Singing, which had helped Alma in her early career. Here she came to the attention of John Schroeder, an A&R manager at Columbia records, who organized a demo version of "Birth of the Blues".

Norrie Paramor, who was already heavily involved producing records for both Cliff Richard and Gene Vincent, heard the demo and was amazed to discover that the powerful, deep voice belonged to the fourteen year old Helen Shapiro.

Paramor signed the teenager to the Columbia label and began searching for a suitable song for her debut single. Rather than take the path of so many others and produce a cover version of an American hit, Paramor had John Schroeder and fellow writer Mike Hawker write a song especially for Helen – the teenage protest song "Don't Treat Me Like A Child".

The song was recorded at the famous Abbey Road studios in January, 1961 and the young Helen had to borrow a record player from a neighbour to listen to her promotional copy, as her family didn't own one.

By March, 1961 the record had climbed to number 3 in the UK charts and her next release "You Don't Know" did even better, reaching number 1 at the end of June, making her the youngest ever female performer – at just 14 years and 316 days old – to hit the top of the charts.

Her next record, the infectious "Walkin' Back to Happiness" also reached number 1 in October, 1961 but from then on her chart career started to slide, with her last top ten hit being "Little Miss Lonely" which peaked at number 8 in July, 1962.

At the end of 1963, Helen Shapiro began a national tour of Britain. Among the supporting acts was a group that was destined to shake up the British – and indeed the worlds – music scene in a way never seen before. The Beatles had arrived and the world would not be the same again

Chapter Six: – Top Gear

"And the Watkins Copicat echo chamber"
(Al Stewart – Class of '58)

The popularity of British rock 'n' roll which developed in the second half of the 1950's was by and large generated by the peculiarly British music called skiffle, as performed by the likes of Lonnie Donegan and artists such as The Vipers skiffle group.

The great attraction of skiffle music was its simplicity; no great musical skill was required and the instruments used were, shall we say, very basic. A common skiffle band line up would consist of a guitar or banjo player, a bass made from a tea chest, a broom handle and a single string, a washboard played with thimbles on the fingers and perhaps an harmonica or kazoo, a simple wind instrument.

Many of the instruments used by skiffle players were in fact home made from common items found around the home – washing machines were a rarity in 1950's Britain, as were vacuum cleaners, so washboards and broom handles were readily available. If a harmonica was not readily available, then the old standby of paper and comb could be used.

But guitars and banjos were harder to fabricate, even though many attempts – some successful – were made by aspiring musicians. For the most part, the guitar was the most expensive item in a skiffle band.

In the years following the Second World War, Britain was faced with enormous debts to America resulting from the American aid shipments, warships and other war materials received during and immediately after the war under the Lend Lease agreement of 1941.

The post war economy in Britain – when rationing was the norm and money was scarce – together with the embargo on imports from American to help ease the war debt, made American guitars almost impossible to obtain, so would-be guitarists turned to European guitar manufacturers instead.

There were relatively few guitar manufacturers in Britain in the early 1950's but one manufacturer stands out as being remarkably popular with British guitar players of the time - Grimshaw Guitars.

Grimshaw and Sons was formed in 1933 by Emile Grimshaw, a noted banjo player, composer and author, who had previously worked for the Clifford Essex Company. He had given banjo lessons to private students and sold them banjos made by Robert 'Bob' Blake of Finchley, London.

With his own company, Emile Grimshaw initially sold banjos designed by Blake, but as demand increased the manufacturing was moved to the Houghton factory in Birmingham – Houghton's being a manufacturer of banjos for other firms, which would subsequently be sold under the designer's name and trademark.

As demand for guitars increased, Grimshaw and Son established their own guitar workshops in 1940 and by 1947 had established a reputation as a manufacturer of high quality guitars, a reputation which would continue for the next two decades, extending their range from purely acoustic guitars to semi-acoustic electrified models.

Grimshaw guitars were in demand among the players in the mid 1950's and were used by a number of famous and not so famous guitarists of the time, such as Bruce Welch (during his pre-Shadows days), Jimmy Currie (who played with Tony Crombie and his Rockets and later with Lonnie Donegan), Joe Brown, Tony Sheridan and Joe Moretti (who later played the unforgettable riff on Johnny Kidd And The Pirates biggest hit "Shakin' All Over").

In the 1960's and 1970's Grimshaw guitars would also be famously used by Pete Townshend (The Who), Frances Rossi (Status Quo), Spencer Davis (The Spencer Davis Group) and Alvin Lee (Ten Years After).

As well as providing experience for Emile Grimshaw, the Clifford Essex Company has a further claim to fame as being the company that made the guitar featured on the classic recording of the James Bond Theme.

Back in 1893, two men, Clifford Essex and Alfred D. Cammeyer opened a shop and teaching studios in Piccadilly, London, where they sold banjos and zithers made for them by Temlett, Weaver, Wilmshurst and Windsor.

Within three years the two had opened their own workshops and were employing fourteen craftsmen to manufacture their own brand of instruments. However, disagreements arose between the partners, and the firm of Essex and Cammeyer was dissolved in 1900.

Clifford Essex then formed his own company under his own name and began selling banjos which were initially made for him by outside manufacturers including Richard Spencer in London and Houghton's in Birmingham. Soon Essex once again had his own factory and in 1915, he bought the machinery and stock, together with the craftsmen employed by Richard Spencer when the latter died.

It was in 1936 that the company moved premises to Shaftesbury Avenue in London, became a limited company and changed name once again to become Clifford Essex & Son Ltd. It was under this name that the famous Clifford Essex Paragon De Luxe, plectrum style, double 'F' hole acoustic guitar was made in 1939.

The guitar, now known worldwide as the 'James Bond' guitar, was used by Vic Flick in 1962 to record the instantly recognizable theme music for the *James Bond* series of films.

The Second World War diminished the supply of the raw materials required for musical instruments and skilled craftsmen who had not been called up for national service were rare, with the result that Clifford Essex & Son Ltd. was forced into liquidation in 1942.

However, all was not lost as the former managing director, A. P. Sharpe soon reformed the company under the name of Clifford Essex Music and at the end of the war was able to entice the former master luthier, Marco Roccia, to join him in the new venture. Under Roccia the range of instruments was expanded to include classical guitars, plectrum guitars and mandolins.

The company thrived under Sharpe's leadership, but his death in January, 1968 proved a mortal blow and within a few years the company had folded once again. However in 2007 the company was re-established under the leadership of Clem Vickery as Clifford Essex Music Co. Ltd. and is once again manufacturing world class musical instruments.

But British manufacturers alone could not hope to satisfy the growing demands and guitars flooded in to Britain, the majority in the form of Höfner, Framus and Egmond guitars.

The most popular European guitars among the skiffle players came from the German company Höfner, which had been established by Karl Höfner in Schönbach in Bohemia – part of the Austro-Hungarian Empire – in 1887 as a manufacturer of violins.

At the time Schönbach was a regional centre for musical instrument manufacturers, with many of the local population being of German descent. After the First World War Schönbach found itself now part of the newly formed Czechoslovakia with the break up of the old Empire, however, this was no obstacle to the company, which expanded into the export business, giving Höfner a world-wide reputation as manufacturers of high quality stringed instruments.

The company's range of instruments was expanded, firstly to include violas, cellos and double basses and, in the 1930's, steel strung guitars with arched backs and tops and known locally as 'Schlaggitarren'.

The rising tensions immediately prior to World War Two had a dramatic effect on the company as the Sudetenland, an area of

Czechoslovakia including Schönbach, was annexed by Germany in 1938. The two Höfner sons, Joseph and Walter, were conscripted into the German army in 1939 and the Höfner factory, by then with around 300 employees, was forced to produce wooden based army items such as crates and wooden boot soles.

However, the greatest threat to the company came after the end of the war, as Schönbach was now located in Czechoslovakia and German companies were nationalized and placed under the control of state appointed administrators. The Höfner Company itself was merged into a state-owned instrument making concern known as Cremona.

To make matters worse, the Czechoslovakian government, under what was known as the Benes Decrees, began expelling the unpopular Germans from the Sudetenland. As a result the Höfner family – including the founder, Karl and his eldest son Joseph – joined the exodus towards what remained of Germany to the west.

The youngest Höfner son, Walter, was released from a prisoner of war camp at about the same time and found himself in Möhrendorf in Bavaria. It was to this area that another German business man, Fred Wilfer, had connived to lead a group of skilled craftsmen from Schönbach – even managing to smuggle out a small supply of instrument quality tonewood.

Wilfer, as the leader of the group of craftsmen, realised that he had a responsibility to find work for his workers, and contacted Walter Höfner with a proposal to go into partnership to found a new instrument making company at Möhrendorf – Wilfer could provide the craftsmen, while Walter had the necessary expertise in instrument manufacture.

Because Walter was still under suspicion of being involved with the Nazis, no formal agreement could be made, but a verbal agreement was made between Wilfer and Walter's wife, Wanda, and on January 1, 1946 the 'Franconian Musical Instruments Manufacture

Fred Wilfer' company – known as Framus – was founded in an old army barracks in Möhrendorf.

By 1948 the remainder of the Höfner family had also made their way to Möhrendorf and had cleared themselves of the taint of any Nazi involvement. Eager to re-establish the Höfner company name, Walter split from Framus, although the parting of the ways was not without some disagreements. Fred Wilfer moved his Framus operations to Baiersdorf in October, 1948 and later to Bubenreuth in mid-1954.

The Höfner family started their new operations in another ex-army barracks in Möhrendorf in January, 1949 and by 1950 their catalogue was able to describe a full range of stringed musical instruments.

However, it soon became apparent that the old barracks location was too small to accommodate the rapidly growing business, so the family took the bold step of not only constructing a new factory from scratch, but also to include accommodation for their still loyal workers from the old establishment at Schönbach – in effect to build a complete new small town.

A suitable location was found at the small village of Bubenreuth and the foundation stone for the new estate was finally laid in October, 1949. Amazingly, the Höfner company was again producing musical instruments in the new factory by early 1951.

During the early 1950's production steadily increased, but it was the skiffle and rock 'n' roll explosion in the mid 1950's which caused the demand for guitars to skyrocket. The factory at Bubenreuth was expanded and guitar production suddenly became more than 50% of the total output – something totally unpredicted at the start of the decade.

The range of models produced by Höfner increased to include semi-acoustic and solid body electric guitars as well as a range of bass guitars – the latter included the famous Höfner 'violin bass' favoured by Paul McCartney.

Höfner guitars were imported into the UK through the Selmer company, which also imported other European and American guitars such as the Swedish Hagstrom and the American Gibson, although as stated previously, American guitars were often prohibitively expensive or simply not available in the UK until after 1961, when the embargo on American brands was lifted.

Figure 10 - Colorama Guitar
The famous Red Colorama from 1962.
Photo courtesy Steve Russell

Selmer often re-badged Höfner and other European guitars and sold them under their own brand names, so that for example the famous 'red guitar' referred to in Al Stewart's Class of '58 and the

Colorama from the same song was actually a Höfner 160 series European model re-badged as a Colorama.

Among the most popular of the Höfner guitars sold in the UK through Selmer were the archtop Congress and Senator models, available only through Selmer and introduced in 1953. Hank Marvin (The Drifters and later The Shadows) started his musical life with a Höfner Congress, as did so many others of the time. In fact, the Congress model was the best seller of the Höfner range, continuing in the Selmer catalogue up to the middle of the 1970's.

As rock 'n' roll increased in popularity in Britain, teenagers and aspiring rock 'n' roll musicians could catch tantalising glimpses of exotic guitars in films and newsreel reports of American rockers. Guitars such as Gibson and Gretsch arch top semi acoustic guitars, as played by artists such as Bill Haley and Eddie Cochran seemed out of this world – both figuratively and literally – to struggling musicians in Britain.

The closest that early British rock 'n' roll guitarists could come to these exotic and unattainable gems were the models offered by Grimshaw – the SS Deluxe was very popular – and the Höfner models imported from Germany by Selmer, such as the single cutaway President or Committee models. Less popular were the Framus model semi acoustics, although Framus appear to have had a more loose agreement as regards importation into the UK than Höfner.

Framus guitars were largely imported into the UK by Boosey & Hawkes, although the latter did not have a monopoly on the importation of Framus. Instead, Framus would deal with just about any importer in the UK, which led to the Framus guitars being sold in the UK in the late 1950's under a variety of names, such as Broadway and Columbian.

The Egmond guitar story goes back to the Second World War, when the three sons of Uilke Egmond – Gerard, Dick and Jaap – joined their father in his music business in Eindhoven and made the decision to start manufacturing guitars, mandolins and banjos in their own right.

Egmond are perhaps better known for the quantity of their guitars rather than the quality and this is reflected in their prices which, in the late 1950's was around 10% of the prices asked by the likes of Fender and Gibson.

The Egmond guitars were sold under a number of brand names in Europe in their heyday. Names such as Wilson, Caladonie and Miller were actually re-branded Egmonds, but perhaps the most well known of the Egmond guitars was sold in Britain under the Rosetti brand name.

Among the famous guitarists who started their careers with an Egmond guitar are future Beatle George Harrison, whose first guitar was an Egmond Toledo, sold in Britain as a Rosetti 276 and Brian May from Queen, who also started on an Egmond Toledo.

But the classic rock 'n' roll guitar at the time, seen in many video clips and TV performances of the late 1950's is the single cutaway, semi acoustic archtop along the lines of the Selmer(Höfner) President.

While an acoustic guitar is fine for small clubs and coffee shops – the usual venue for a skiffle group – the increased popularity of rock 'n' roll called for greater volume. An acoustic guitar needs some form of amplification to produce that rock 'n' roll sound, so a market began to develop for quality amplifiers to connect to those guitars.

Once again, Selmer comes in to the picture. In December 1947, Selmer had taken over R.S. Amplifiers, a small company in west London that had been producing small PA amplifiers under the name Truvoice, so Selmer was in an ideal position to expand production from PA amplifiers to guitar amplifiers to suit their imported semi-acoustic guitars.

Figure 11 - Selmer Truvoice Amplifier
1962 Selmer Truvoice Selectortone Automatic amplifier.
Photo courtesy Steve Russell

These were introduced to the ever demanding market in the early to mid 1950's under the Selmer-Truvoice brand name. Models such as the Selmer-Truvoice TV8, TV10 and TV15 combination amplifier and loudspeaker – the '8', '10' or '15' referred to the nominal size of the amplifier output in watts – were soon becoming popular among guitarists.

Power output was understandably low – around eight to fifteen watts – but this was sufficient at the time to enable the guitar to be heard over the drums. There are rumours that the first combination amplifier and loudspeaker used by the pre Beatles Quarrymen was a Selmer U12 combo, consisting of an amplifier of around twelve watts and two loudspeaker cabinets, which could be clipped together for easy transportation, together with a microphone.

Probably the name most associated with British amplifiers is VOX, and indeed the classic VOX AC30 amplifier had become the ultimate guitar amplifier by the middle of the 1960's. But VOX amplifiers only appeared on the scene under that name in 1957 with the AC2/30 model.

Prior to that date we must go back to 1950, when Tom Jennings, an ex Royal Engineer during the Second World War, formed Jennings Musical Instruments and opened a small music shop in Charing Cross, London.

A year later the Jennings company started to sell a small portable amplifier, under the brand name Ultravox, which could be used as a guitar amplifier. By 1954 the company had begun developing a monophonic electric keyboard, also rather confusingly known as the Ultravox and a small volume controlling foot pedal, the first product to be sold under the VOX brand name.

By 1956, Jennings had started producing a small range of guitar amplifiers to meet the demand started by rock 'n' roll. These were designed in-house by Derek Underdown, who had joined the company back in 1951.

Tom Jennings was not totally satisfied with the amplifiers being produced by his company, which by now had changed its name to Jennings Music Industries – better known as JMI – and contacted an old army friend, Dick Denney, who had been working independently on a guitar amplifier design. Denney agreed to join JMI at the end of 1957 to continue his development work there.

In January, 1958, JMI started to market the first Denney designed amplifier, the VOX AC15, which soon became a favourite among guitarists with its twelve-inch speaker and crisp, clean sound. Early users of the VOX AC15 included Bert Weedon and, in 1959, Cliff Richard's backing group The Shadows.

1960 was a big year for the VOX brand. Driven by the demand for more powerful guitar amplifiers, the company doubled up the popular AC15 model and produced the classic AC30/4, which boasted twin twelve-inch speakers and two channels – including one with vibrato/tremolo effects.

In July the same year The Shadows reached number 1 in the UK charts with their great instrumental hit "Apache", which gave even greater exposure to their VOX AC15's. However, the group demanded more volume and by the end of 1960 had upgraded to three of the more powerful AC30/4 models.

Figure 12 - VOX AC30 Amplifier
The classic VOX AC30 amplifier, used by many groups including The Shadows and, later, The Beatles. This model from 1961.
Photo courtesy Steve Russell

JMI did not sit back and enjoy their success, however, and by the end of the year had upgraded the AC30/4 to include a third channel, giving a total of six inputs. Naturally enough, the new version was known as the VOX AC30/6.

The VOX success continued throughout the early and mid 1960's, highlighted by The Beatles selection of VOX amplifiers in 1962.

Another name familiar to those of us lucky enough to have lived in those heady early days of rock 'n' roll is Charlie Watkins. The history of Watkins guitar amplifiers and effects goes back to 1949, when ex-seaman Charlie Watkins opened a record shop in Tooting Market, in London with his brother Reg.

Figure 13 - Watkins Dominator Amplifier
The Watkins Dominator had twin ten-inch speakers and a nominal seventeen watts output. This model from 1961/62.
Photo courtesy Steve Russell

The Watkins brothers moved their business to Balham (gateway to the east, according to comedian Peter Sellers) in 1951 where they expanded into guitar and accordion sales – an interest which led Charlie into a lifelong fascination with the electric guitar and the develop-development of the first Watkins amplifier, known as the Westminster, introduced in 1954, with a power output of around ten watts.

By 1956 the range had expanded to include the less powerful – just six watts output – Clubman and the legendary V-front Dominator. The Dominator, with it's seventeen watts output, twin ten-inch loudspeakers arranged in a V-formation to give better sound spread, twin channels and four inputs together with a tremolo made it the perfect combo for the times before the beat boom of the 1960's made it uncompetitive against the screams of the audiences.

Figure 14 - Watkins Copicat Echo Unit
The classic echo unit of the time. This model from 1961.
Photo courtesy Steve Russell

But probably the most well-known contribution to the music business by Charlie Watkins is the Watkins Copicat echo unit. In 1958, after two of his customers returned from a trip to Italy, where they had seen the Italian tenor Marino Marini use an echo device on stage to great effect, Charlie became intrigued and started playing around with a gramophone motor and spare tape recorder re-cord/playback heads.

The result was the Mark 1 version of the Copicat stage echo unit and to prove the viability of the unit as a commercial device, Charlie had 100 units made. The demand was amazing, with a queue forming outside his shop before opening time and all 100 units selling in just the first day – with the first unit going to a certain Johnny Kidd.

Charlie Watkins – as Watkins Electric Music, or WEM – went on to become the name behind some of the biggest master-slave PA units used in the biggest pop and rock festivals in the 1960's and 1970's. His units were the first to break the 1,000 watt level during the 1967 Windsor Jazz, Pop and Blues festival, when audiences at the outdoor concert were treated to Peter Green's Fleetwood Mac playing through a WEM Wall of Sound system.

There were, of course, other amplifier brands that became popular during the 1950's – names such as Elpico, Grampion and Dallas could be found in smaller clubs and used by those with limited finances due to their low price and even lower output. For the most part these amplifiers were designed to be used with record player decks and tape recorders, but could, with a little ingenuity, be used to produce a small amount of volume when used with an electric guitar.

Towards the end of the 1950's there was another revolution in guitars – the hollow body guitar was challenged by the new, solid body models. Musicians and fans alike were amazed to see the sleeve of the 1957 released Buddy Holly and the Crickets LP record "The Chirpin' Crickets" with Buddy holding a sunburst solid body guitar – the Fender Stratocaster.

Of course every guitarist in the land wanted a guitar like Buddy's, but the American embargo – and the price – put the instrument out of reach of just around everyone.

The only option for British guitarists was to once more look to their home grown and European guitar makers for affordable copies of this Holy Grail. And there was no delay in making supplies available.

As with the acoustic and semi-acoustics of the mid 1950's, Höfner quickly had a range of sold bodied electric guitars in the market place. The Höfner range, with models such as the 160, 161 and 162 models had already been introduced in 1956, but in Britain the budget level solid guitar sold by Selmer was the iconic Colorama, introduced in 1958.

It was almost as if Henry Ford had been involved with Selmer. Instead of Ford's promise to Model T purchasers that they could have any colour they liked, as long as it was black, the Selmer version was (almost) that prospective buyers could have any colour Colorama guitar they liked, as long as it was red.

There were in fact blue Coloramas available, but red was the colour of choice for the great majority – it somehow had that excitement and vibrancy that the music demanded. The Colorama continued in production through until the middle of the 1960's and remained a favourite among many professional and amateur groups.

But Selmer imported not only Höfner and Höfner-based, rebadged models. An important addition to the Selmer range was made in 1958 to 1959, when Selmer began importing and selling a three pick-up, solid bodied guitar from Czechoslovakia, made under the trade name of Resonet, by the Drevokov Co-Operative, based at Blatn.

Drevokov – who also made furniture – had apparently managed to import a Fender Stratocaster from America just a couple of years previously, and a certain Mr. Ruzicka had been inspired by this guitar to develop the Resonet Grazioso model.

Selmer changed the name to the more appealing – to British guitarists at least – Futurama and began selling these guitars in the UK for a just about attainable price of 55 guineas.

Apart from the price, the Futurama's main appeal was the advanced electrics hidden under the large white scratchplate. While the Fender Stratocaster also had three pick-ups, the guitarist could only, at that time, select three combinations of pick-ups, while the Futurama, with piano type toggle switches for each pick-up, could achieve a mix of seven different combinations.

The Futurama also featured an advanced tremolo unit which, like the Stratocaster unit had individual string adjustments on the bridge saddle and had individual springs for each string. The similarity with the Stratocaster did not extend to the headstock, however, as this retained the traditional three a side tuners.

In 1959, the three main driving members of the Drevokov guitar manufacturing arm – Mr. Ruzicka, together with the production manager, Josef Rika and the design engineer, Mr. Vlek, left the company to join the Czechoslovak Music Instruments – known by its Czech initials as CSHN – company in Hradec Kralove.

CSHN carried on the manufacture of solid bodied guitars as the production of the Resonet Grazioso at the Drevokov Company closed down in 1959. Their first guitar in the series was a twin pick-up model named the Jolana Star I, which Selmer imported and, naturally enough, marketed under the name Futurama II for just 25 guineas.

A three pick-up model was also produced by CSHN, named the Neoton Star II and this became the Selmer Futurama III, selling at 45 guineas. By 1960 the headstock had changed to the more attractive six-on-a-side style favoured by Fender.

The Futurama range from Czechoslovakia lasted until the early 1960's but was then replaced by a new range, confusingly also called Futurama, but with the suffix De Luxe. These new guitars were actually made by the Swedish guitar manufacturer Hagstrom[9] and continued to be sold by Selmer until the latter half of the 1960's.

There were few manufacturers in Britain who could compete with the European imports, but a number of British manufacturers made a significant impact during the late 1950's and 1960's.

In addition to producing the classic 1960's VOX AC30 guitar amplifier, JMI, under the brand name of VOX also saw the potential in the solid bodied guitar market and, in late 1959, began selling guitars under the imaginative name of VOX Solid Body. These were outsourced and bear a quite striking resemblance to the Japanese Guyatone models of the time, although they were manufactured for VOX by a cabinet maker in Shoeburyness in Essex.

By 1960 VOX had expanded their range of guitars to include the Apache, Stroller and Clubman models which were based on the still unobtainable Fender solid bodied models, complete with bolt-on necks. However, it was in 1962 that VOX introduced the revolutionary looking Phantom model.

The Phantom pentagonal body shape was the result of a design commissioned by Tom Jennings from the London Design Centre and immediately aroused great interest. VOX followed up the Phantom a year later with the Mark VI, which also had an unusual body shape which gave it the nickname the teardrop guitar.

Charlie Watkins' company not only imported guitars from Europe and made amplifiers and effects units, but at the end of the 1950's Charlie's brother Reg began toying with the idea of making his own solid bodied guitars.

However, Reg was beaten to the punch to be the first British solid bodied guitar maker by the John E Dallas company, who introduced their Tuxedo model, just a few days before Reg unveiled the Watkins Rapier in 1959. In 2012 a Dallas Tuxedo, reputedly found in the attic of John Lennon's old home in Liverpool, sold at auction for almost $7,000.

The Watkins Rapier was available in a range of models, such as the Rapier 22 and Rapier 33, with the numeric suffix giving an indication of the number of pick-ups – and no, the Rapier 22 did not have twenty-two pick-ups, just two, and the Rapier 33 had just three pick-ups. There was also a Rapier 44 model and all variations were available to suit left or right handed guitarists.

Following closely behind Watkins and Dallas came the legendary Jim Burns, who would score major headlines in 1964 when his Burns Marvin model was selected by Hank Marvin, no less, as a replacement for his equally famous red Fender Stratocaster in a major coup for the company.

Jim Burns started off working in partnership with Henry Weill, producing Burns-Weill guitars, but the two parted company after less than a year, each pursuing the path of guitar manufacturing greatness.

While Weill started marketing his guitars under the Fenton-Weill brand name, with models such as the Dual master (twin pick-ups), the Triplemaster (three pick-ups) and the Amazon (which was also made for Hohner and sold as the Hohner Apache), Jim Burns started producing his own guitars.

Early Burns guitars boasted model names such as the Artist, the Vibra Artist and the Sonic, but it was the 1961 Black Bison which became the most expensive British solid bodied guitar, reflecting Jim Burns's refusal to downgrade quality for economy.

In fact the Black Bison sported many technical innovations among its black shiny construction, including four ultra-sonic pick-ups sharing split sound circuitry and a unique worm and gear wheel truss rod system for the neck.

So expensive was the Black Bison to manufacture that only 50 units were actually made before the guitar was redesigned as a three pick-up model with a bolt-on neck and marketed as just a Burns Bison, which became one of the most iconic solid bodied guitars of the early 1960's.

However, the British and European manufacturers were fighting a losing battle to try to stem the incoming tide of Fender, Gibson and other American guitars when the flood gates opened in the middle of the 1960's.

Of course, rock 'n' roll is not all about the gyrations – both physical and vocal - of the singer or the scorching guitar breaks; rock 'n' roll is all about solid beat and that comes mainly from one source – the drummer.

In the period just after the First World War, popular drumming was in its infancy and most drum shells were made of single plywood, painted or simply varnished and most fittings were nickel plated. The drum 'kit' as we know it today was a long way off in the future.

In fact it would not be until the mid 1930's that the drum kit was developed, largely thanks to Gene Krupa, who performed the first recorded drum solo on the 1937 recording by Benny Goodman of "Sing, Sing, Sing".

Krupa was also responsible for the development of several standard components of the modern kit, in conjunction firstly with the Slingerland Drum Company with the development of adjustable tom-toms and secondly with the Avedis Zildjian Cymbal Company with the growth of modern cymbals.

In the mid 1950's the demand for big bands and orchestras diminished considerably and more modern styled drum kits, with chromed fittings and easier transportability for travelling between gigs became the ideal. Manufacturers such as the American based Slingerland, Ludwig and Gretsch companies and the British based Premier company became the choice of many rock 'n' roll drummers from then on.

Chapter Seven: – Behind The Scenes

"And there's a man who's a producer, and he puts their record out"
(Al Stewart – Class of '58)

As good as the musicians were, and however awesome they sounded on stage, it was in the recording studios that their sound would be captured for posterity and that would be bought by the teenagers hungry to listen to the music in their own homes.

These days it is possible to put together a home recording studio that far surpasses in capability the majority of the big name studios in the 1950's and early 1960's. Digital equipment has made it possible to re-record over mistakes made, or change tempo or even fix individual false notes at the click of a mouse or press of a button.

While today's artists may spend months in the recording studios, the practice in those early days was to rehearse and polish a performance well before entering the studios. Many of the classical pop and rock 'n' roll songs of the early days were recorded in one take, with strategically placed microphones around the studio. If a mistake was made, well, the whole process was repeated.

Sound recording goes back to Thomas Edison, with his early attempts to reproduce sound in July 1877. Edison's equipment was very simple – a telephone speaker, a diaphragm, an indenting stylus and some paraffin coated paper – but the basic concept remained in place for several decades.

Edison had found out that by converting sound waves into a mechanical force, he could record these as indentations on his paper, and later replay the sounds by reversing the process – forcing the stylus to repeat the initial movements and mechanically amplifying the resulting energy to a sound.

However, despite progressing from paraffin coated paper to tin foil, Edison was unable to replay his recordings more than a couple of times before they became worn out and unintelligible.

By 1886, the team at the Alexander Graham Bell's Volta laboratory, in Washington DC, which included Charles Tainter and Chichester Bell, improved Edison's process by recording on to wax cylinders and called their machine a graphophone.

Two years later Edison, too, had switched to the longer lasting wax cylinder and improved his machine, which he called a phonograph, by joining the recording and playback diaphragms together and powering the machine by an electric motor, to give a constant speed.

The same year, Emile Berliner, a German immigrant who had moved to America in 1870, announced his 'talking machine' which he called a gramophone. For the first time in commercial production, this machine used a flat disc instead of the cylinders previously used by Edison and Bell.

A new concept was introduced in 1889, when the American engineer Oberlin Smith, who owned an engineering shop in New Jersey, described a process where, he believed, it would be possible to take the electrical signals from a telephone microphone and, by applying these to a steel wire, produce variations in magnetism along the wire, resulting in a recording which could be replayed by reversing the process.

Unfortunately for Smith he never patented his idea, and it was left to the Danish engineer Valdemar Poulsen to take Smith's concept and develop the first magnetic wire recording system in 1898.

But mechanical sound recording was still the main target for improvements. By making a negative metal master copy from the original wax recording through electroplating, it was possible to mass produce copies of the recording.

Gradually the flat discs became the standard, mainly for two reasons – it was easier to duplicate a recording onto a flat disc and also, as the disc has two sides as opposed to the single recording surface of the cylinder, it was possible to double the recorded content.

However, the wax discs being used were fragile, clumsy and short-lived, as well as having very limited frequency response. A new recording medium was needed to enable further progress.

The answer came with the development of the first plastic materials, and soon production had switched from wax to celluloid and shellac, both much longer lasting than wax and able to reproduce frequencies at the higher and lower ends of the spectrum.

After the First World War, many improvements were made in sound recording and it was in 1925 that the development of electrical methods of recording began to take over.

Rather than using purely mechanical means to move the recording cutter to make the impressions in the master record, Western Electric Company engineers Joseph Maxfield and H. Harrison realized that the innovations being made in the field of telephony could be utilized to develop a system of electrical recordings. A condenser microphone, producing electrical current variations, could have this electrical output amplified electrically and the resulting increased current could be used to drive the recording cutter head. To playback the recorded sound, a stylus mounted in a magnetic cartridge could reproduce the electrical impulses, which in turn could be amplified electrically and used to drive a loudspeaker.

Although records produced by the new electrical method could be replayed on the older mechanical playback machines, the results were less than impressive and the full benefits were not obtained unless replayed on the Western Electric Orthophonic machine.

By the mid-1930's the new electrical system had virtually taken over, and improvements continued to be made at an ever increasing rate, especially during the war years when technology enjoyed an enormous boost.

In 1948 Ampex marketed the first professional quality magnetic tape recorder, a breakthrough which was to revolutionize the music recording process, Although music was still largely sold to the public in the form of discs, the initial recordings were now made on tape before a metal master was produced from which the vinyl discs were pressed.

Tape recording made it possible to re-use the recording medium and, more importantly, record more than one track simultaneously on the same tape, although Les Paul, the famous guitarist and sound recording innovator, had experimented with multi-tracking using acetate discs back in the 1930's.

By 1950 shellac 78 rpm records were beginning to be replaced by the new 45 rpm vinyl discs, and long playing, 33⅓ rpm started to make an impact. It was now possible to faithfully reproduce, on disc, an artist's performance to sell to the eager public.

The recordings made in the late 1950's and early 1960's have a clarity, urgency and crispness that modern recording engineers strive to attain. Remember that modern effects processors, multi-track recordings and other modern devices were just not available to those pioneer recording engineers.

Much of the success of the engineers from those days was due to close attention to the placement of their microphones and the quality of the equipment used – in other words, great techniques and great equipment. But they were also great innovators and experimenters, always searching for new methods to achieve a sound that they could hear only in their heads.

When American rock 'n' roll records began to arrive in Britain, sound recording engineers there would scratch their heads and wonder how some of the effects on those discs had been obtained.

How were they to know, however, that prior to the recording of "Rocket 88" in Sam Phillips' studio in Memphis, the guitarist Willie Kizart's amplifier had fallen off the roof of the group's car and ruined the speaker cone. Rather than try to hide the distorted tone that the amplifier now produced, Sam Philips packed the cone with crumpled newspaper and boosted the amplifier's sound, giving a fuzz guitar effect.

Or how would a British recording engineer know that the great reverberation produced on the early Bill Haley and His Comets' recordings was partly due to the domed ceiling in the Decca studio in New York – which just happened to be in a former ballroom known as the Pythian Temple.

Indeed, many of the smaller recording studios in America at the time realized that a perfectly built recording studio, well insulated from outdoor interferences, produced a dry, unnatural sound and reverted to placing speakers and microphones in stairwells, tiled bathrooms or other areas where they could get intriguing echo effects.

Another, more technical, reason for the biting, incisive sound on those early American rock 'n' roll recordings compared with their early British equivalents is in the actual process for cutting the master records.

Many British recording studios were more accustomed to the refined sounds of the easy listening music they had recorded up to that point, and were cautious with sound levels and the power amplifiers used to drive the actual cutting heads. Most of the studios were in fact using simple ten or twelve watt amplifiers for the purpose, whereas in America the amplifiers were often ten times more powerful.

As a consequence, the grooves in the American record were cut much deeper, allowing the playback stylus to reproduce the louder and high and low frequencies better, so the records would have an immediate impact when played on a juke box or over the radio.

But British recording engineers and producers caught on quickly. Enter the man who was to become a legend among British rock 'n' roll producers, Norrie Paramor.

Norrie Paramor spent much of his time during the Second World War acting as a piano player in his role as an entertainment officer for the Royal Air Force, but after the war began to concentrate on arranging and conducting, rather than performing.

Paramor joined EMI records as a conductor with his own light entertainment orchestra, but by 1952 he had graduated to becoming the A&R manager for the company's Columbia label and quickly established his reputation by signing acts such as the trumpeter Eddie Calvert and the singer Ruby Murray, who had a huge hit for the label in 1955 with "Softly, Softly".

But by 1955 the British music industry began the changes that would drive the industry for the next decades. Skiffle had arrived and shortly after rock 'n' roll in the form of the avuncular Bill Haley and His Comets took the country by storm.

Haley's success, enhanced by his tour of Britain, forced EMI executives to begin searching for home-grown talent to compete with the American acts. Their initial search was for groups in the same style as Haley, but as other stars such as Buddy Holly and Elvis Presley sharpened the edge of Haley's music style, the British companies widened their search for local acts capable of merging the two styles.

In 1958, Norrie Paramor found what he was looking for with Cliff Richard and his backing group, then called The Drifters. Impressed by Cliff's looks and musical ability, Paramor initially wanted to sign just the young singer and use him with The Ken Jones Orchestra, but the tightness and sound of The Drifters – soon to be The Shadows – convinced Paramor to keep the combo together.

Cliff Richard's first single was, according to Paramor's wishes, going to be the softer "Schoolboy Crush", but in the evening of July

24, 1958 in the recording studio – Studio number two at Abbey Road – the engineer in charge, Malcolm Addey, who was just a few years older than Cliff, was disappointed in the song and arrangement, including as it did The Mike Sammes Singers providing sugary backing.

Addey, a generation younger than Paramor, was looking for something punchier that the teenagers could relate to. Ian Samwell, The Drifters rhythm guitarist, had come up with a song, "Move It", which Paramor had described as 'rubbish'.

However, Addey was convinced and, after waiting for The Mike Sammes Singers to leave, proceeded to record the song, with session guitarist Ernie Shears, playing a Höfner President guitar providing the stinging intro and the first two bars of the rhythm before switching to providing the fills behind Ian Samwell's rhythm as he took over.

Addey's philosophy was to record exactly what he could hear coming from the speakers in the studio, and that's just what he did. After a false start, the song was recorded in its entirety, with no editing or after effects applied.

TV producer Jack Good heard the record, fell in love with the guitar intro and Cliff's Americanized vocals and booked Cliff for his TV show *Oh Boy!* – and the rest, as they say, is history.

Norrie Paramor was equally impressed by Addey's handling of the recording session and soon the two became a formidable partnership in the recording side of Cliff Richard's career. Not only Cliff, but also that of his backing group, The Shadows.

Now convinced of the potential of Cliff Richard and The Shadows as a rock 'n' roll outfit, Paramor took the unprecedented step, unheard of in Britain or America, of recording the group's first LP record live in front of a studio audience.

The LP was recorded in February, 1959 in the Abbey Road number One studios, to accommodate several hundred screaming fans, and was a great success, reflecting once again Malcolm Addey's philosophy of recording just what could be heard. The approach would be repeated just four years later by another legendary producer, George Martin, when he produced the Beatles first LP.

Gradually, however, sales of the rock 'n' roll songs began to slip in favour of the softer, pop orientated songs and Norrie Paramor was able to steer Cliff Richard in the direction he'd first envisaged, a more romantic style in the mould of the American Rick Nelson.

Another British record producer who was to become a legend at EMI was Walter J. Ridley, who had discovered and signed Alma Cogan in the beginning of the 1950's to EMI, under the HMV label.

Ridley had been busy during the war helping to organize radio broadcasts for the 'Forces Favourite' Vera Lynn and, oddly enough, the radio programme for the ventriloquist Peter Brough, *Educating Archie*.

After the war, with the British entertainment business slow to catch up on the Americans, EMI became one of the outlets for American labels such a RCA-Victor, MGM and Columbia, and marketed records by American artists of the calibre of Frank Sinatra and Guy Mitchell.

EMI management signed Ridley as a producer whose main task was to build up the company's HMV label – at the time seen as a label devoted to classical music – with a range of British recording artists.

Beginning with Alma Cogan, Ridley quickly signed up British artists Max Bygraves – with whom he had worked during the *Educating Archie* radio series – Donald Peers and the band leader Joe Loss.

But HMV was also the label under which Elvis Presley's RCA-Victor early releases were sold in Britain, and Ridley was greatly impressed, not only with the technical recording expertise demonstrated on these records, but the likely impact this new music was likely to have on British teenagers.

Ridley also thought that the British musicians of the time were incapable of playing in the rock 'n' roll style he was hearing on those early Elvis recordings, despite the success his fellow EMI producer Norrie Paramor was enjoying with Cliff Richard and The Shadows.

By 1959 Ridley had signed a group which he thought had the potential to achieve that American sound – Johnny Kidd And The Pirates. Although the first few records didn't make a huge impression, in 1960 the chart topping "Shakin' All Over" confirmed Ridley's faith in the group. Such was the strength and power of this record that many could not believe that it was a British recording.

Unfortunately EMI, along with many of the recording companies of the time, didn't quite know how to handle the phenomenon of British rock 'n' roll, with the result that Johnny Kidd And The Pirates were restricted largely to recording more pop orientated songs, although a few rhythm and blues numbers recorded during this time attest to the group's unfulfilled potential.

Apart from the EMI group, the other major player on the British popular recording scene during the 1950's was Decca records, who were fortunate enough to have signed Hugh Mendl as a record producer in 1950.

Early in his career at Decca, Hugh Mendl worked with performers such as Winifred Atwell – he produced her memorable "Black and White Rag" – and the American Josh White, who had moved to England in 1950 as he had been blacklisted in America for suspected communist activities.

In 1952, Hugh Mendl was appointed as the manager for the Decca subsidiary Brunswick – with another appointee, Dick Rowe being placed in charge at the Capitol label.

Inspired by the traditional jazz movement starting in Britain at the time and continually searching for new talent for his Brunswick label, Mendl began frequenting the traditional jazz clubs, in particular the 100 Club in London.

It was here that he spotted The Chris Barber Jazz Band and signed them to his label. On July 13, 1954, The Chris Barber Jazz Band was in the middle of their first Decca recording session under Mendl's production. As the jazz group ran out of suitable material to record, the group's banjo player, Lonnie Donegan, suggested that they 'do a bit of skiffle.'

The result was a recording of the Leadbelly song "Rock Island Line." Decca were unsure what to do with the mixture of folk, traditional jazz, blues and country music, and shelved the recording for more than a year, but finally released it in 1956, whereupon it was an immediate chart success.

Spurred on by the success of Lonnie Donegan, Mendl moved on to the burgeoning sound of rock 'n' roll, and signed Tommy Steele for the Decca label.

Mendl's fellow appointee from 1952, Dick Rowe, also achieved fame at Decca, although his main claim to fame lies in his rejection of demo tape by The Beatles, claiming that 'four piece groups with guitars are dead'.

Dick Rowe first achieved success with the singing group The Stargazers, with whom he reached the top of the UK charts in 1953 with the song "Broken Wings" and, when he later became head of A&R for Decca, followed up with acts such as Lita Rosa and Dickie Valentine before working with the Larry Parnes discovery Billy Fury.

Rowe left Decca for a short while to work with Joe Meek at Top Rank records, but soon rejoined Decca and produced a number 1 UK chart hit for ex-Shadows Jet Harris and Tony Meehan with "Diamonds" in January, 1963. He later went on to sign several Liverpool groups as the Mersey beat phenomenon took over, but his biggest signing for Decca was in May, 1963, when, following a recommendation from George Harrison of The Beatles, he auditioned and signed The Rolling Stones.

The producer who did take on The Beatles after Dick Rowe had rejected them was George Martin, who had joined EMI in 1950, following a time spent working for the BBC's classical music department. Martin's first job at EMI was as an assistant to Oscar Preuss, then head of the Parlophone label.

Parlophone was considered the poor relation of the EMI family when compared with the more popular Columbia and HMV labels and indeed ranked only just above the Regal Zonophone label, which was the label carrying Salvation Army Band records.

Preuss retired in 1955, and George Martin took over at Parlophone. He was, at 29, the youngest of the label managers and had already taken a keen interest in the technological changes in the recording process that were taking place, such as the use of tape mastering and overdubbing.

With little in the way of popular artists coming to the Parlophone label. George Martin concentrated instead on non musical artists, such as Peter Ustinov and Peter Sellers, then a mainstay of *The Goons* radio show.

In the early years of skiffle and rock 'n' roll, Martin was beaten to the punch by Hugh Mendl at Decca, who managed to sign first Lonnie Donegan and then Tommy Steele. However, Martin was successful in signing The Vipers skiffle group, who had at some stages of the line-up included not only Tommy Steele, but also future Shadows Hank Marvin and Bruce Welch.

Martin's skill as a record producer was his ability to communicate with his artists in a way unlike the other main producers of his era. While Norrie Paramor liked to dictate the direction of his artists such as Cliff Richard towards a softer image and Walter J. Ridley was known to communicate with his protégée Johnny Kidd through memos rather than face to face, Martin preferred to record his artists as they were and not as he would like them to be.

Although he will always be associated with The Beatles, it was this skill that enabled both he and other artists to achieve such phenomenal success in the 1960's. In 1963 records produced by him for artists such as the Beatles, Gerry and the Pacemakers, Cilla Black and The Hollies spent an incredible 37 weeks in the number 1 position in the UK charts.

However, Martin's contract with EMI ended in 1965 when his attempt to renegotiate his salary to include a small producer's bonus failed. Martin left Parlophone and EMI to set up his own independent production company AIR with his assistant Ron Richards and two other ex-EMI producers. He continued to work with The Beatles however up until 1969.

A producer who could successfully claim fame as both songwriter and producer was Tony Hatch. The son of a musical family – his mother was a pianist – Hatch was encouraged in his musical leanings and was enrolled in the London Choir School when he was just ten years old.

Although he could have enrolled in the Royal Academy of Music, Hatch preferred to work in the music industry and obtained a job as a tea boy with the Tin Pan Alley firm of Robert Mellin Music instead.

His career blossomed as he began writing his own songs and he soon joined Top Rank records – a subsidiary of the Rank Organisation – where he worked closely with the Decca A&R manager Dick Rowe.

Leaving Top Rank for a short period while he served his time with the Coldstream Guards during his period of national service, he returned to the music industry in 1959, when he released a cover version of the pianist Russ Conway's hit "Side Saddle".

His composing career gained a boost when his song, "Look For A Star" was recorded by Garry Mills – who had supplied the singing voice for actor Jess Conrad in the TV play *Rock A Bye Barney* – and became a top ten hit for Top Rank in 1960. The song was also featured in the film *Circus Of Horrors*.

When Top Rank was sold to EMI in 1961, Tony Hatch found himself working instead for the Pye label and it was here that both his song writing and record producing talents were fully developed under the eagle eye of his boss Alan A. Freeman – not to be confused with the radio DJ Alan 'Fluff' Freeman.

Hatch began working closely with one of Freeman's protégées, Petula Clark, and produced Clark's comeback record, "Sailor" in 1961. A number of successful compositions and record productions followed, not only for Petula Clark, but also American stars such as Connie Francis and Pat Boone.

Hatch went on to have an extremely successful collaboration with The Searchers when the beat boom overtook Britain, writing and producing the group's hit "Sugar And Spice" and also working with artists such as David Bowie. He is also fondly remembered as the co-composer, with his wife Jackie Trent, of the theme tune for the Australian hit soap opera TV series *Neighbours*.

Another producer who eventually set up his own business was the legendary Robert George "Joe" Meek. Meek, who could neither sing nor play a musical instrument, served an apprenticeship in the Royal Air Force as a radar technician, following on from his childhood interest in radio and electronics.

Joe Meek trod that fine line between insanity and genius and, like Phil Spector in America, in his quest for that special sound that only he could hear in his head, took many pioneering steps in sound recording, including the manufacture of several innovative 'magic boxes'.

After a short spell working for the Midland Electricity Board following his RAF training, Meek found work as an audio engineer for a company producing programmes for Radio Luxembourg run by Denis Preston called Record Supervision Ltd. Preston's company signed a licensing deal with Pye records and it was during this period that Meek first began record production.

When Preston founded Lansdowne Studios in 1956, Meek followed as recording engineer. By this time Meek had established a small recording studio in the bedroom of his flat in Notting Hill and, working in there – and also after hours at Lansdowne Studios – began producing records by little known artists. Meek managed to sell one of these recordings, by the Larry Parnes discovered singer Lance Fortune and entitled "Be Mine" to Pye records and the record reached number 4 in the UK charts.

However tensions developed between Preston and Meek and in January, 1960 Meek left to form his own company, Triumph Records, in association with William Barrington-Coupe and financed by the business man Wilfred Alonzo "Major" Banks.

Triumph's target audience was specifically teenagers, an unlikely market at the time as the majority of records were purchased by adults. The label's first record was numbered RGM 1000 – the initials from Joe Meek's real name – by a group Meek himself discovered, Peter Jay and The Blue Men, entitled "Just Too Late".

Many of the Triumph releases sank without trace, despite the massive publicity. An exception was the Michael Cox recording of "Angela Jones", which featured heavily on the Jack Good TV show *Boy Meets Girls* and reached number 7 on the UK charts in June, 1960.

However, being a small independent company, Triumph could not keep up with demand for the record, limiting potential sales. Disappointed by this, and suffering from an acute lack of money for the company, Joe Meek left Triumph, but retained his connection with Banks by jointly forming a new company, RGM Sound Limited, with Banks as company director and Meek as recording director.

Meek continued with his recordings of little known artists and attempted to sell these to the larger labels, to get around the distribution problems he had faced at Triumph. RGM productions were available through labels such as Pye, Top Rank, Decca and HMV and met with limited success, until Meek finally managed to produce a record which captured the 'Meek' sound.

In August, 1961, the Joe Meek produced, John Leyton song, "Johnny, Remember Me" reached number 1 in the UK charts. Arranged by Charles Blackwell, the so-called 'death song' moves ahead with a relentless pace, driven by the rhythm guitar played, according to most observers, by session man Eric Ford, and enhanced by an atmospheric refrain sung by the classically trained Lissa Grey.

Initially banned by the BBC because of the morbid references to 'the girl I loved who died a year ago', lyricist Geoff Goddard changed the line for the recorded version to 'the girl I loved and lost a year ago' but the BBC still refused to add it to their play list.

Undeterred, Meek managed to have the song included in the ITV crime series *Harpers West One*, in which John Leyton had a starring role at the time. This exposure caused a rush for the record and it was a smash hit, cementing Meek's position as a front-line producer.

The follow up record, "Wild Wind" had similar Meek ingredients, with the echoing, somewhat spacey backing, and managed to reach number 2 in the UK charts in October the same year.

But in 1962, Joe Meek produced what is likely to be the record for which he is most remembered, "Telstar", credited to The Tornados.

In fact The Tornados, who were then the backing group for Billy Fury, only managed to put down a basic backing track and some guitar work before Larry Parnes dragged them away from the recording studios to fulfil their contract and tour with Billy Fury. It was left to Joe Meek and Geoff Goddard to build the track up to the final release standard.

Inspired by the launch of the first communications satellite, Telstar 1, on July 10, 1962, Meek added his own space sound effects to the intro and fade out of the record, while Geoff Goddard played the unforgettable melody on a clavioline and added some wordless vocals towards the end of the record. Meek worked his magic by speeding up the whole recording and adding reverberation and compression effects.

Figure 15 - The Tornados
Originally Billy Fury's backing group, The Tornados found fame with a string of hits produced by Joe Meek, starting with 'Telstar' in 1962
© Victoria and Albert Museum, London

Although The Tornados, on first hearing the finished result, reputedly called it 'crap', the record went on to become one of the biggest selling instrumental records in pop music history. Released in Britain on August 17, 1962 on the Decca label, the record had reached number 1 on the UK charts by the end of the month, where it stayed for five weeks. It stayed in the UK charts for no less than six months.

By Christmas, 1962, "Telstar" had conquered the American Billboard charts and had reached the charts in seventeen different countries.

Joe Meek continued producing records in his own, inimitable style, even with the rise of Mersey beat. His next big success was in June 1964, with The Honeycombs record "Have I The Right", which featured more unusual Meek recording techniques.

Once the basic recording had been put down, Meek arranged for the band members to tramp up and down the stairs in his apartment building in time with the music. Meek recorded this through five microphones fastened to the stair banisters with bicycle clips. He also had a microphone beaten directly with a tambourine to get the drum effect only he could imagine.

Finally the whole recording was sped up and put through some of Meek's own specially designed reverberation and compression units. Once again a Meek recording reached number 1 on the UK charts, despite fierce competition from the likes of Manfred Mann, The Searchers, Billy Fury and Freddie and The Dreamers. The record also made the top five in the American Billboard charts.

Although his records were great chart successes, Joe Meek never received the royalties he deserved during his lifetime. His most successful record, "Telstar" was the subject of a plagiarism claim from the French composer Jean Ledrut, who asserted that four bars from the "Telstar" melody had been lifted from a film score he had written in 1960 for the film *Austerlitz*.

With the plagiarism claim filed just a couple of months after the chart success of the tune in March, 1963, the British Copyright Society froze all royalties due until the case was decided.

The case dragged on for five years and the outcome was ruled in favour of Ledrut, who was awarded £8,500 – a considerable sum in those days. The remaining royalties were unfrozen, but by then it was too late for Joe Meek.

Unfortunately Joe Meek was, as previously noted, somewhere between genius and madman. It was as the latter that, on February 3, 1967 – the eighth anniversary of the death of Buddy Holly – he grabbed a shotgun belonging to Heinz Burt – bass guitarist with the Tornados – and shot his landlady before turning the gun on himself.

Chapter Eight: – The Composers

"And every song was short and sweet and every beat was fast"
(Al Stewart – Class of '58)

During the skiffle years in Britain, the majority of the songs were re-workings of traditional folk or blues songs, and you need to dig deep to find the original composer – for example, the song "Rock Island Line", a worldwide hit for Lonnie Donegan in the early months of 1956, has its origins in the recordings made by John Lomax in the Gould, Arkansas prison back in 1934.

The song was later popularized by Huddie Ledbetter – better known as Lead Belly – who first recorded it in 1937, almost twenty years before Lonnie Donegan made it such a hit. Other favourites from the skiffle era include "Pick A Bale Of Cotton", "Cumberland Gap" and "Railroad Bill" – all usually listed as traditional compositions.

Later in his career Lonnie Donegan moved away from skiffle towards the more British music hall style, when he recorded the song "My Old Man's A Dustman" – co-written by Donegan and his manager at the time Peter Buchanan, and comedy songs such as "Does Your Chewing Gum Lose Its Flavour".

Another local musician and songwriter to achieve prominence during the skiffle years was Wally Whyton, founder of The Vipers skiffle group. His composition "Don't You Rock Me, Daddy-O" was recorded by both The Vipers and Lonnie Donegan, and both versions had top ten chart success with the song in January, 1957.

However, it was not until rock 'n' roll hit the British music scene that local composers began to gain real recognition, although the standard recipe for a chart success was still to record a cover version of an American hit.

Britain's first successful rock 'n' roller, Tommy Steele, is listed as composer of several of his early hits, including "Happy Guitar", "Elevator Rock" and "Teenage Party". Along with Lionel Bart and Mike Pratt, the Bart/Pratt/Steele combination gained composition credits for Tommy Steele's first hit record, "Rock With The Caveman" as well as "Butterfingers" and "Handful Of Songs".

Of the trio, Lionel Bart was to achieve the greatest success as a songwriter. Born Lionel Begleiter in Stepney, East London, his father worked as a tailor. After serving in the Royal Air Force, Lionel changed his surname to Bart, reputedly after passing St. Bart's hospital on top of a London double-decker bus, and started his song writing career in amateur theater.

In 1953, while working for the Unity Theatre in London, Bart began writing comedy songs for the BBC radio programme *The Billy Cotton Band Show*, but it was in 1957 that his career took off with his collaboration with Mike Pratt and Tommy Steele on the soundtrack for the film *The Tommy Steele Story*, when the trio reputedly wrote the twelve songs called for in the script in just seven days.

Lionel Bart is also credited with the composition of one of Cliff Richard's biggest early hits, "Livin' Doll", and he also provided songs for Adam Faith ("Easy Goin' Me") and Anthony Newley ("Do You Mind") before he gained international success with his musical stage production *Oliver!* in 1960.

The production was the first modern British musical to make a successful move to Broadway. Future musical stars to appear in the London production included both Steve Marriot (later to gain fame as a member of The Small Faces), and Phil Collins, destined to become the drummer in Genesis.

Bart followed the success of *Oliver!* with the musical *Blitz* in 1962 before gaining more accolades with his theme for the James Bond film *From Russia With Love* in 1963. However, the ill-fated musical *Twang* – based on the legend of Robin Hood – signalled the end of his musical career.

Bart's song-writing partner for the Tommy Steele hits, Mike Pratt, had less success than Lionel Bart in a musical career, but gained fame through his acting, appearing in many TV series, including *No Hiding Place*, *Z-Cars* and *Jason King* but is probably best remembered for his portrayal of the private detective Jeff Randall in the TV series *Randall and Hopkirk (Deceased)* alongside Kenneth Cope as the ghost of Marty Hopkirk.

One of the first wave of successful British rock 'n' roll songwriters was Jerry Lordan, who, like many of his generation, served time in the Royal Air Force. On leaving the air force, he tried his hand at several musical ventures, including being one half of the unsuccessful duo Lee and Jerry Elvin, who recorded one song on the Fontana label before sinking without trace.

While working for a London advertising agency, Lordan managed to transform several of his songs into demos, which found their way to Decca records. One his songs, "A House, A Car And A Wedding Ring" was recorded by an up and coming singer Mike Preston and although it did not make any impact in the charts, it did convince Decca to give Lordan another chance.

His second offering to be accepted by Decca was featured in the Anthony Newley film *Idle On Parade*, in which Newley played the role of a pop star and sang the Lordan song "I've Waited So Long". The song ultimately reached number 3 in the UK charts in May, 1959 and launched Jerry Lordan's career, both as a singer and composer.

Despite having two of his songs recorded and released by Decca artists, Lordan was signed by EMI and subsequently had several records released as a singer on the Parlophone label, three of which reached the UK top 40 at the end of 1959 and early in 1960.

However, Jerry Lordan is probably best known for his instrumental offering, "Apache", which was first recorded by the British guitarist Bert Weedon but his record label, Top Rank, was slow to release Weedon's version. At the time The Shadows, Cliff Richard's backing group, were searching for a suitable 'B' side for their fourth solo record, a Norrie Paramor suggestion of the traditional song "Quartermaster's Stores".

The Lordan tune was suggested, despite having been recorded, but not released by Bert Weedon and quickly became the 'A' side of The Shadows release. Top Rank reacted by releasing the Bert Weedon version, but while The Shadows reached number 1 in the UK charts in August, 1960, the Bert Weedon version managed only a couple of weeks in the UK charts, topping out at number 24.

"Apache" was also a success in America, but by yet another artist, the Danish guitarist Jorgen Ingmann, who took the tune to number 2 in the Billboard Hot 100.

The Shadows scored more chart successes with Jerry Lordan's "Wonderful Land" and "Atlantis" and Lordan also supplied the ex-Shadows duo Jet Harris and Tony Meehan with two chart entries in "Diamonds" and "Scarlett O'Hara" in 1962 and 1963.

TV was the medium that brought British rock 'n' roll to the forefront, in particular the programmes developed by Jack Good. It was from one of Good's later programmes *Drumbeat* that not one, but two successful British songwriters appeared, John Barry and Les Vandyke.

John Barry was the son of the owner of a small chain of movie theatres and developed an early interest in music and films. He studied the piano as a boy, but turned to the trumpet in his teen years. He carried on this interest during his time spent in national service in the army, where he played trumpet when he was assigned to a musical unit.

Barry was heavily influenced by the use of music to enhance films, in particular films such as *The Third Man* and *A Song To Remember* and he tried his hand at musical arranging as well as playing, even undertaking a correspondence course developed by one of the bandleader Stan Kenton's arrangers, Bill Russo.

On completion of the course, Barry considered himself ready for a new musical career and had the confidence to send some of his arrangements to England's top bandleaders of the time, including Ted Heath, Johnny Dankworth and Jack Parnell.

Although Dankworth agreed to use two of Barry's arrangements, it was Jack Parnell who made the suggestion that Barry form his own musical group. Liking the idea, Barry called on several of his ex-army colleagues and by 1957 had formed The John Barry Seven.

Assisted by Barry's father and his connection with film theatres, the group started a short tour of theatres in and around York, and it was while appearing at the York Rialto that they were spotted by the impresario Harold Fielding, who offered the group the spot as backing group for Tommy Steele during his extended season at Blackpool.

These concerts in turn led to appearances on firstly the *Six-Five Special* TV programme, then on to become a permanent part of the Jack Good produced *Oh Boy!* By the time *Drumbeat* appeared on TV screens in 1959, the group was established as top class, having released several records under their own name as well as backing well known pop acts on TV.

Drumbeat featured the young pop singer Adam Faith, together with a singing group called The Raindrops, whose members included Johnny Worth. John Barry, Adam Faith and Johnny Worth soon developed a profitable partnership, with John Barry writing the arrangements for Faith's records and The John Barry Seven providing backing both on TV and on tour. Johnny Worth provided the song which was to kick start Adam Faith's career, "What Do You Want?"

Johnny Worth was born Yani Panakos Paraskeva Skoradalides in Battersea, south London and initially trained as a draughtsman before his national service. However, he had decided to make a name for himself as a singer and, having changed his name to Johnny Worth, began singing in various local pubs and clubs.

Worth managed to score a TV appearance, where he was spotted by the wife of the bandleader Oscar Rabin, who convinced her husband to sign Worth to the band.

Worth made several records with the Oscar Rabin band on the Columbia and Oriole record labels before joining up with singers Jackie Lee and Vince Hill to form The Raindrops.

Although gaining some success as a singer, Johnny Worth also had aspirations to become a songwriter and, while appearing on *Drumbeat*, he showed his composition "What Do You Want?" to John Barry. Barry liked the song, as did Adam Faith, who agreed to record it.

With Barry's sensational arrangement of pizzicato strings coupled with Adam Faith's unusual vocal style, the record had an immediate impact and rocketed to the top of the UK charts in November, 1959, staying in the charts for a total of nineteen weeks.

As Worth was still under contract with Oriole records at the time, he became concerned over possible conflicts and although he retained the name Johnny Worth for his singing career, adopted the name Les Vandyke – supposedly taking the first name from The John Barry Seven's pianist Les Reed and the surname from the name of his local telephone exchange.

Under his new pseudonym, Les Vandyke wrote not only the follow up record for Adam Faith – "Poor Me", which reached number 1 in the UK charts in January, 1960 – but went on to write a further six top ten UK chart hits for Faith over the next two years.

Les Vandyke went on to build a successful career as a songwriter, providing a number 1 UK chart hit for Eden Kane with "Well I Ask You" in June, 1961 as well as Kane's follow up top ten successes, "Get Lost" and "Forget Me Not". In addition his songs were recorded by a number of artists including Marty Wilde, Petula Clark, Anthony Newley and John Leyton.

Not to be outdone by Vandyke, John Barry also achieved great success as a composer, writing, arranging and conducting the score for the Adam Faith film *Beat Girl* before reaching a world-wide audience with his arrangement and enhancement of the simple Monty Norman melody which became known as the "James Bond Theme".

The theme was first featured in the original James Bond thriller *Dr. No* and the opening signature riff is played by The John Barry Seven's guitarist Vic Flick on a Clifford Essex Paragon Deluxe guitar from 1939 connected to a VOX AC15 amplifier.

Barry went on to provide the scores and arrangements for the next James Bond film, *From Russia With Love*, although the title song is credited to Lionel Bart. Barry's later film successes included *The Lion In Winter*, *Midnight Cowboy*, *Born Free*, *Out Of Africa* and *Dances With Wolves* earning him five Academy Awards and four Grammy Awards.

While many performers of the time, particularly in the mid to late 1950's were quite happy to leave the song writing to specialists – and the songwriters in turn were equally happy to have others perform their efforts, there were several artists who preferred to combine both activities. Well before Lennon and McCartney set the trend of both writing and performing their own material, Billy Fury was determined to do both.

It was indeed the combination of Fury's looks, singing ability and his own compositions that encouraged entrepreneur Larry Parnes to sign him in the first place when he met him in Marty Wilde's dressing room for an audition in October, 1958.

During the audition, Fury sang two of his own compositions, "Maybe Tomorrow" and "Margo" for Parnes, and these two songs were the 'A' sides of the first two singles released by Billy Fury on the Decca label, reaching number 18 and 28 respectively in the UK charts.

With bad publicity resulting from his over-zealous stage act giving negative reviews in the press, Fury's next two singles failed to make the charts, but he hit back with another of his own compositions, "Colette", which reached number 9 in the UK charts in March, 1960.

This success prompted the release of his first long playing album, *The Sound Of Fury*, which featured Joe Brown on guitar but more importantly, all ten of the songs were Fury compositions.

By 1961, Billy Fury – or more rightly said, Decca records – had changed his style more towards ballads and away from rock 'n' roll. The style suited his voice and his ambitions to be regarded as not just another rock 'n' roll singer, and he scored major chart successes with "Halfway To Paradise" and his biggest hit, a reworking of the standard "Jealousy" which reached number 2 in the UK charts in September, 1961.

The success of his new style moved him away from recording his own compositions, but he will always be remembered as a fine songwriter as well as an impressive singer.

Other artists to score chart success with their own compositions during those frantic years included Marty Wilde, whose recording of his own composition "Bad Boy" proved to be one of his biggest chart hits, reaching number 7 in December, 1959.

After their initial success with the Jerry Lordan classic, "Apache", the Shadows too were able to record some of their own compositions, such as "Geronimo" – composed by Hank Marvin – "Shindig" and "Foot Tapper" – credited to Hank Marvin and Bruce Welch – and "Theme For Young Lovers", a Bruce Welch composition.

Chapter Nine: – The Trad Jazz Revival

"And every paper in the land said rock and roll won't last"
(Al Stewart – Class of '58)

It seemed that pop music at the beginning of the 1960's had set-tled down from the frenetic pace of those early rock 'n' roll years, but look more closely and you would see the signs of a return to the music that started it all off before skiffle – traditional jazz, or Trad Jazz.

Just after the Second World War, traditional jazz was extremely popular in Britain. Jazz artists such as Humphrey Lyttleton led the transformation from the pre-war styles of boogie-woogie and big band blues to the more New Orleans influenced jazz.

Humphrey Lyttleton came from the unlikely background of an Eton College education, where he first started his love affair with jazz, playing trumpet after being inspired by the great Louis Armstrong and Nat Gonella. On leaving college, Lyttleton spent some time working at the Port Talbot steel works in south Wales, before joining the army and serving as a second lieutenant in the Grenadier Guards.

Lyttleton's first recorded radio broadcast was on VE Day – May 8. 1945 – when he was heard on a BBC radio recording playing his trumpet from a wheelbarrow during the celebrations, the start of a long successful career in music.

After the end of the war, Lyttleton attended the Camberwell Art College, where he teamed up with The George Webb Dixielanders jazz band, before forming the Humphrey Lyttleton Band in 1948.

The band signed with Parlophone records and recorded a string of 78 rpm records, including the first-ever British top 20 chart success by a jazz band when his own composition "Bad Penny Blues" reached number 19 in the UK charts in June, 1956 – a record produced, incidentally by a young Joe Meek.

Lyttleton began to feel stifled by the limitations of the Trad jazz style and gradually moved to include other styles such as Latino-American and African influences in his music, touring America in 1959 with Thelonious Monk and Anita O'Day. In later years he worked successfully with Helen Shapiro on various jazz projects and became a familiar voice hosting jazz programmes on BBC radio.

While Humphrey Lyttleton moved away from the Trad jazz format, other musicians were embracing Trad, including Ken Colyer, who can with some degree of certainty lay claim to having a great influence on the birth of skiffle music in Britain.

Ken Colyer taught himself to play both guitar and trumpet and, being influenced by the Dixieland style of jazz, joined the Merchant Navy in 1945 at the age of just 17. He travelled to America, where he could hear at first hand the greats playing in New York and Montreal.

In 1949, on his return to England and after resigning from the Merchant Navy, Colyer formed The Crane River Jazz Band along with fellow Trad jazz enthusiast Monty Sunshine, playing New Orleans style jazz.

Colyer left the band in 1951 and rejoined the Merchant Navy. During his nautical travels, he jumped ship in Mobile and made his way to New Orleans, where he sat in with the local bands during his time ashore. However, Colyer was soon arrested and deported for his desertion of his ship.

On his second return to England in 1953, Colyer got together with another couple of Trad jazz musicians, Monty Sunshine – from The Crane River Jazz Band - and Chris Barber, to form Ken Colyer's Jazzmen.

As had happened previously with The Crane River Jazz Band, Colyer incorporated a 'band within a band' segment in the performances, which was intended to demonstrate to the audience the origins of jazz through a guitar based highly rhythmical interpretation of American folk music.

When Colyer left in 1954 because of musical differences with trombonist Barber, the band regrouped and become known as The Chris Barber Jazz Band – which also featured the banjo and guitar playing Lonnie Donegan.

The Chris Barber Jazz Band achieved considerable success with its first LP record, called *New Orleans Joy*, which sold 60,000 copies in the first month of release alone. Despite objections from Decca, for whom the album was recorded, the band included some of the Lonnie Donegan 'skiffle' numbers on the LP.

Looking to capitalize on the success of the album, in 1955 Decca began releasing individual titles from the LP as singles – one of which was the Lonnie Donegan skiffle version of the Leadbelly song "Rock Island Line". The rest, as they say, is history.

Shortly after this success, Donegan left The Chris Barber band, although Barber did continue to play on several Donegan releases after the split. The Chris Barber Jazz Band continued to enjoy success without Donegan and reached number 3 in the UK charts in February, 1959 with their recording of the Sydney Bechet tune "Petite Fleur".

As well as being a Trad jazz fan, Barber also had an appreciation of American blues music and was largely instrumental in the arrangements of British tours in the late 1950's by artists such as Muddy Waters, Sonny Terry and Brownie McGhee and Big Bill Broonzy – artists who were to become major influences in the musical careers of young British musicians such as Peter Green, John Mayall and Brian Jones.

Trad Jazz continued to enjoy success in Britain during the late 1950's and early 1960's, despite the impact of skiffle and then rock 'n' roll, with bands such as Barber's and the reformed Ken Colyer's

Jazz Band, while not achieving great heights in the UK charts, proving popular among live audiences and radio and TV shows.

But as the rock 'n' roll movement began to fade away, Trad Jazz once again began to be a major influence in Britain. A graduate of the original Ken Colyer's Jazzmen, Somerset's Acker Bilk was destined to record one of the most successful jazz hits with his hit "Stranger On The Shore" in 1961.

Born Bernard Stanley Bilk, the nickname 'Acker' came from the local Somerset word for mate or friend. Bilk studied piano while at school, but claimed that the continuous practice interfered too much with his sporting activities – perhaps he would have been better off practicing, as his outdoor activities resulted in the loss of his two front teeth and half a finger. However, he later claimed that these accidents had an influence on his musical style when he later adopted the clarinet as his musical instrument of choice.

Suffering from an uninspiring job at the local cigarette factory after leaving school, Bilk then joined the Royal Engineers for his national service, and was sent to Egypt's Suez Canal Zone. It was there that he first learned to play the clarinet on a dilapidated instrument picked up in a local bazaar by a fellow engineer, but who decided it was not for him.

On his return to England, Bilk continued playing clarinet with local bands and in 1951 briefly moved to London to join The Ken Colyer jazz band. However, he soon returned to his beloved west country, where he formed his own band, initially named The Chew Valley Jazzmen, but soon renamed as The Bristol Paramount Jazz Band.

In a move destined to be followed a decade later by many British bands, the band gained a six-month booking in a beer bar in Düsseldorf, Germany, where they played seven nights a week, seven hours each night, tightening and honing their style, including the fashionable bowler hat and striped waistcoat stage attire for which they later became famous.

Following on from the trip to Germany, the band returned to London and played successfully in the burgeoning jazz club scene. Bilk began composing his own tunes and it was with one of these, "Summer Set" – a pun on their home county's name Somerset – co-written by Bilk and the band's pianist Dave Collett, that Mr. Acker Bilk and The Paramount Jazz Band scored their first UK chart success in 1959, reaching number 5 in the UK charts.

The band had previously had several recordings released on the Pye record label, but these had failed to chart and it was with the Columbia release of "Summer Set" that the band made their breakthrough. A string of releases followed, picking up on the rekindled interest in Trad Jazz, and the band enjoyed top ten successes with "Buona Sera" in 1960 and "That's My Home" in 1962.

But it was in 1962 that the band enjoyed their greatest success with the Bilk composed "Stranger On The Shore". Originally entitled "Jenny", in honour of his daughter, the tune was renamed to fit in with a TV series where it was intended to be the theme song.

The TV exposure, coupled with the lush string arrangement provided by The Leon Young String Chorale combined with Bilk's low end, vibrato filled clarinet, ensured chart success and the record topped at number 2 in the UK charts in November, 1961, remaining in the charts for an amazing 55 weeks. Bilk also achieved the distinction of being only the second British recording artist – after the wartime favourite Vera Lynn – to have a number 1 record on the American Billboard charts.

As the Trad revival continued, Acker Bilk continued to score successes up until 1962, but nothing equalled the runaway success of "Stranger On The Shore" – which Bilk often laughingly referred to as his old-age pension.

Slightly less well known than the bands of Ken Colyer and Chris Barber, Terry Lightfoot nevertheless contributed to the growth in popularity of Trad Jazz in the late 1950's, and at various times his band included such future luminaries as the trumpeter Kenny Ball and drummer Ginger Baker – the latter set to gain fame later in the 1960's a member of the power trio Cream, alongside Eric Clapton and bassist Jack Bruce.

Terry Lightfoot taught himself to play clarinet while still attending the Enfield grammar school, where he joined the school jazz band. Encouraged by the growth of Trad Jazz, he formed his first band, The Wood Green Stompers in 1952 when just 17. The band's name reflects the loose camaraderie of the band's style – in Lightfoot's mind the music was there to be enjoyed with a laugh and a smile.

As with many of his contemporaries, Lightfoot completed his national service in the Royal Air Force and on leaving in 1955, he formed The Terry Lightfoot New Orleans Jazzmen and the group turned professional two years later. With tight performances and an obvious enjoyment in their music, the band quickly became in demand and toured with Lonnie Donegan and the American star Slim Whitman.

The highlight of the band's career was the inclusion in the film made to capitalize on the boom in Trad Jazz, appropriately named *It's Trad, Dad* in which they performed the song "Tavern In The Town", which became the band's greatest chart success, reaching the lower end of the top 50 in May, 1962.

Although never able to repeat this chart success, The Terry Lightfoot New Orleans Jazzmen continued to feature prominently on radio and TV throughout the 1960's, making appearances on the BBC radio programme *Saturday Club* and six seasons with the popular TV comedians Morecambe and Wise.

Another strong influence in the revival of the Trad Jazz movement in the late 1950's and early 1960's was the trumpeter Kenny Ball. Ball left school when he was just 14 to work in an advertising agency, but he spent his free time learning to play the trumpet and was soon playing as a semi-professional with local bands in his home town, Ilford, Essex.

He turned professional in 1953, taking on the trumpet spot in bands led by Eric Delaney and Terry Lightfoot among others before forming his own Trad Jazz band, Kenny Ball and His Jazzmen, in 1958.

In 1961, after a couple of unsuccessful records, the band recorded and released the Cole Porter song "Samantha" which became an immediate hit, reaching number 13 in the UK charts in February that year. The band's next two releases, "I Still Love You All" and "Someday", although reaching the top thirty, failed to have the same impact as their first hit, but in November, 1961 they gained their biggest chart success with "Midnight In Moscow", which peaked at number 2 in the UK charts and the American Billboard charts.

The hit made Kenny Ball and His Jazzmen the most popular of the early 1960's Trad Jazz scene and a string of top 30 hits followed, including "March Of The Siamese Children" – from the musical *The King And I* – "So Do I", and "Sukiyaki". Such was Ball's popularity that he featured on the cover of the prestigious British musical newspaper 'New Musical Express' in July 1962 along with Cliff Richard, Joe Brown, Frank Ifield, Craig Douglas and the American songstress Brenda Lee.

In January the following year, at the peak of the Trad Jazz revival, Kenny Ball and His Jazzmen headlined a major jazz festival – the All Night Festival of Jazz – alongside contemporaries Chris Barber, Acker Bilk and Ken Colyer at London's Alexander Palace. It was, incidentally, the same month that the Beatles released what was to be their first number one hit, "Please Please Me".

As with Terry Lightfoot, Kenny Ball continued to enjoy success during the 1960's, despite the competition from the Mersey Beat boom, which appeared to sweep all before it. The band made regular appearances on radio and TV and appeared in the film *Live It Up* with Gene Vincent in 1963.

One of the more curious musical groups that took advantage of the Trad Jazz revival in the early 1960's was the oddly named Temperance Seven, who, despite the group's name, had nine members.

The group had its roots in the traditional British music hall and successfully managed to combine humour, musical comedy and 1920's jazz in a style that would later become the basis of such groups as The Bonzo Dog Doo-Dah Band and Bob Kerr's Whoopee Band.

The founder members, 'Whispering' Paul McDowell, Philip Harrison and Brian Innes formed the basis of the group at Christmas, 1955 and their light-hearted – to say the least – approach to performances soon attracted like-minded spirits until the group grew to consist on nine members.

The group's name – reputedly supplied by Douglas Gray, a member of the musical surrealistic group The Alberts – was suggested as a convoluted twist on the expression 'one over the eight' – indicating inebriation and intemperance – which was then reversed to 'one under the eight ', giving the number seven, and The Temperance Seven they became.

The Temperance Seven performed dressed in period costume from the 1920's, taking the theme so far as to provide Paul McDowell with a megaphone for his vocal exertions – hence his nickname of 'whispering'.

The group scored a recording contract with Parlophone records in 1961 and with EMI producer George Martin mainly concerned with 'off beat' performers at that time, he was the logical choice to take control of their first record, "You're Driving Me Crazy".

The record, delivered in the group's inimitable style, was a smash hit, reaching number 1 in the UK charts in May, 1961. The follow up, their version of "Pasadena" also did well, reaching number 4 in the UK charts later that year, although subsequent releases did not fare so well and only had minor impacts in the charts.

The Temperance Seven also appeared in the film *It's Trad, Dad!* with Helen Shapiro, Craig Douglas and fellow 'Tradders' The Terry Lightfoot New Orleans Jazzmen, but gradually slipped away into obscurity and disbanded in the mid-1960's as the beat boom took over the musical tastes of British – and the world's – audiences.

Chapter Ten: – The Slippery Slope

"And it's a long, long way from pompadours and doo-wop and payola"
(Al Stewart – Class of '58)

In the early days of the 1960's, you might – if you listened carefully – have heard a collective sigh echo around the country. It was a sigh of relief from parents in Britain who had begun to believe that possibly, just possibly, the danger of rock 'n' roll had passed and life could return to normality.

The youngsters, who just a few years ago had sat with their ears glued to the crackling, fading transmissions emanating from Radio Luxembourg, had matured. They had settled down, got married, perhaps had children of their own and were trapped in the endless cycle of adult life as they struggled to make ends meet. No longer the care-free teenagers of yesterday, they had responsibilities to distract them from the music.

The decade started with an announcement by the BBC executive Donald MacLean, when indicating that the BBC intended to air a new show *Big Beat* – 'Rock 'n' roll is now respectable. The wild stuff has given way to beat ballads and this is what our audiences want to hear.'

Indeed, the rawness of rock 'n' roll had all but disappeared from the UK charts. Songs such as Cliff Richard's "Voice In The Wilderness" and Anthony Newley with "Why" were typical of the musical style that had begun to take over. While Don McLean had announced February 3, 1959 as the day the music died, rock 'n' roll was dealt another devastating blow in April, 1960, with the death of Eddie Cochran in a car crash in England.

The transition from rock 'n' roll to the more palatable – for the non teenagers, that is – easy listening was obviously not a sharp cut-off. Ballads and middle of the road music had continued to chart during the heady days of British rock 'n' roll and many artists who had established themselves during the late 1950's continued their success in the early 1960's.

One such balladeer was the one-time number 27 route bus driver who started off life as Terence Parsons in Shoreditch, London. Better known as Matt Munro, Parsons spent his time while not driving buses in part time singing, including recording advertising jingles for TV commercials.

He also gained valuable experience as a singer with The Cyril Stapleton Orchestra and in 1956 performed on the BBC radio programme *BBC Showband* with Stapleton. The appearance gained him a recording contract with Decca and his first single, "Ev'ry Body Falls In Love With Someone" was released the same year.

Although this, and subsequent releases on both Decca and Fontana records failed to chart, Matt Munro came to the attention of George Martin at Parlophone records in 1958. Martin, who was gaining a reputation at the time for his comedy record productions, was working with the comedian and member of The Goons on a satirical LP record called *Songs For Swinging Sellers*.

Martin was looking for a contribution to the Seller's album – a spoof on the style of Frank Sinatra – and Matt Munro fit the bill perfectly. Munro sang "You Keep Me Swingin'" for the album and his no-nonsense performance – billed on the record as performed by Fred Flange – gained him a recording contract with Parlophone.

His first single for the label failed to chart, but the next release, "Portrait Of My Love" reached number 3 in the UK charts in December, 1960. Further top ten hits followed in 1961 and 1962 and in 1963 Munro achieved international recognition with his performance of the Lionel Bart composition "From Russia With Love", which featured in the second of the James Bond films of the same name.

In 1957, the American singer Johnny Mathis was extremely popular in the UK and it was almost inevitable that a South African singer resident in Britain should soon become known as 'Britain's Johnny Mathis'.

Born in Port Elizabeth, Eastern Cape in South Africa, Danny Williams – his real name – won a talent contest when just 14 and was rewarded with a spot in the *Golden Cities Dixies* touring show. The show moved to Britain in 1959, where the young Williams came to the attention of the EMI producer Norman Newell, who signed him to the HMV label.

Four unsuccessful single releases in 1959 and 1960 did not bode well for Williams, but he scored minor chart success with his next two releases in 1961 and later that year his version of "Moon River" gave him his first and only number 1 in the UK charts in November, where it remained until well into 1962.

His chart success, although not repeated, did give Williams a role in the Michael Winner produced Billy Fury movie *Play It Cool* in 1962 and the next year saw Danny Williams joining a 20-city tour of the UK with Helen Shapiro – also on the bill for that tour was a promising young group called The Beatles.

While 1962 started with Danny Williams sitting at the top of the UK charts with the saccharine sweet, strings and all, "Moon River", you could also find the likes of Pat Boone with "Johnny Will" and Neil Sedaka with his bouncy "Happy Birthday Sweet Sixteen". The age of the balladeers was certainly in full swing.

Another of the very few young coloured singers in the UK in the early 1960's to score chart success was Kenny Lynch, who had top ten hits with firstly a cover of The Drifters "Up On The Roof" in December, 1962 and again in June, 1963 with "You Can Never Stop Me Loving You".

However, Lynch's main claim to fame as a singer is his interpretation of the Lennon-McCartney song "Misery". Lynch was on the same nationwide tour that featured Helen Shapiro, Danny Williams and The Beatles, during which Lennon and McCartney composed the song with the idea of presenting it to Helen Shapiro.

When Helen Shapiro turned down the song, Lynch took over, producing a much more 'pop' orientated arrangement than that The Beatles themselves would use when they recorded it for their first album. Unfortunately for Kenny Lynch, his version flopped.

Kenny Lynch did however go on to have a reasonably lucrative career as a TV performer and as a composer, gaining co-writer credits with non other than the legendary Mort Schumann for The Small Faces song "Sha La La La Lee".

Even though the balladeers appeared to have commandeered the UK charts in the beginning of the 1960's there were a few glimpses of up-beat music, often derived from somewhat unusual sources.

Back in 1958, the success of Tommy Steele prompted his younger brother Colin – who retained the family surname – to try for a career in show business.

Colin Hicks and his backing group, The Cabin Boys, were signed by Larry Parnes – who else? – and given a recording contract with Pye records. In 1957 the group toured Britain with another Parnes protégé, Marty Wilde and in 1959, without achieving chart success, the group undertook a tour of Italy.

During the tour, the group's recording of Freddy Bell and The Bellboys' "Giddy Up A Ding Dong" became a hit in Italy and at the end of the tour Colin Hicks elected to remain in Italy to build on his success. The backing group, The Cabin Boys, however, decided to return to Britain.

Before their return, however, The Cabin Boy's keyboard player, Mike O'Neill and the bass player, Rod 'Boots' Slade managed to obtain several sets of gladiator outfits used in the 1951 film *Quo Vadis* which had been made in Rome.

On their return, O'Neill and Slade decided to disband The Cabin Boys and set their sights on success with a new group. Because of O'Neill's supposed resemblance to a Roman emperor and with their gladiator costumes in hand, the choice of name was easy – Nero and The Gladiators.

With a recording contract from Decca, the group decided to take the Julius Fucik circus tune, "Entry of the Gladiators" and, shall we say, offer a different interpretation. With a spoken introduction by Slade to set the scene – 'Hey, say there Brutus man, like, here come the gladiators' – and a rocking version of the tune, the record was a great hit, reaching number 37 in the UK charts in March, 1961.

The group's second record in the same year caused controversy. With a change of guitarist from Colin Green – who left to join Georgie Fame's Blue Flames – to Joe Moretti, the group decided to record their version of Edvard Grieg's classic "In The Hall Of The Mountain King" from his Peer Gynt Suite.

Unfortunately the record was banned by the BBC, who stated that 'rock groups may not do rock versions of the classics'. Despite this, and aided by yet more scintillating guitar work by Moretti, the record succeeded in reaching number 48 in the UK charts. However, further success eluded the group and they eventually disbanded in early 1964.

The death of Buddy Holly in that plane crash in 1959 had left an enormous hole in popular music and it was no surprise when a young British singer named Mike Berry combined with the legendary producer Joe Meek to capitalize on the Holly style.

Tribute records were not unknown at the time – the American Tommy Dee had recorded "Three Stars" as a tribute to Holly, Ritchie Valens and The Big Bopper and a cover version by Ruby Wright had made the charts in the UK during 1959 – but Berry's tribute song, entitled rather unimaginatively "Tribute To Buddy Holly" was sung very much in the Holly style and with a Buddy Holly styled backing provided by The Outlaws.

Mike Berry had previously recorded a cover version of The Shirelles song "Will You Still Love Me Tomorrow" – a rather unlikely song for a male singer – with Joe Meek producing, but this had failed to make the charts. Both Meek and Berry were keen admirers of Buddy Holly's work and came up with the idea of the tribute song in 1961.

The song, with the drum rhythm which might almost have been lifted from Holly's hit "Peggy Sue" and Mike Berry's vocal mannerisms reflecting Holly's, managed to reach number 24 in the UK charts, despite concerns that the song could be considered as cashing in on Holly's death.

Mike Berry continued to use the Holly style and he achieved even greater chart success in 1962 with the Geoff Goddard/Joe Meek composition "Don't You Think It's Time", which climbed to number 6 in 1962. However, his singing career foundered after that and he became more familiar to TV viewers as an actor, incidentally appearing with Wendy Richard in the TV sitcom program *Are You Being Served?* He did manage to return to the charts in August, 1980 with collaboration with a former Outlaw, Chas. Hodges and the song "The Sunshine Of Your Smile".

But apart from these brief forays into more up-tempo music, the ballad singers were the rule during the early 1960's. Along with the more mature singers such as Matt Munro and Anthony Newley, even the younger singers seemed to be caught up with the easy listening style.

A young shop assistant named Terry Lewis began to make his mark with his amateur singing outside working hours and it was a dance hall performance with a local group, when he stood in for the group's regular singer that caught the eye of a local entrepreneur, Ray Mackender.

To avoid confusion with the popular American comedian Jerry Lewis, Mackender persuaded Terry Lewis to change his name, firstly to Mark Lewis but shortly after to the more commercial sounding

Mark Wynter. He also organized acting and singing lessons for his new discovery.

The investment paid off and by 1960 Mark Wynter was playing the major cabaret clubs in London, appearing on TV and had obtained a recording contract with Decca.

His first release, "Image Of A Girl" proved popular with his intended female record buying audience and the record reached number 11 in the UK charts. Further hits followed, including a Lionel Bart composition "Kickin' Up The Leaves", and Wynter was voted the Most Promising Newcomer of 1961 by the music magazine New Musical Express.

However, it would not be until Wynter switched record labels to Pye in mid-1962 and came under the umbrella of producer/arranger Tony Hatch that he would achieve his greatest success.

The first record released under his Pye contract was a cover of the American record by Jimmy Clanton entitled "Venus In Blue Jeans" and while the Clanton version was largely ignored in Britain, Wynter's version soared up the charts to peak at number 4 in the UK charts.

The follow-up release, another easy-listening ballad entitled "Go Away Little Girl" was almost as successful when it reached number 6, but further releases did not fare as well as the beat boom began to bite in the UK charts. Apart from a number 12 chart placing with "It's Almost Tomorrow" in 1963, Wynter's lightweight ballad style could not compete commercially with the new sounds and despite regular releases throughout the 1960's further chart success eluded him.

Back in 1959, Emile Ford had entered and won a talent contest, which led to a recording contract with Pye records. It was no wonder then that James Little, a friend of Emile Ford's step brothers, George and Dave Sweetman – members of Ford's backing group The Checkmates – was encouraged by the group to enter the same contest a year later.

History repeated itself, and James Little duly won the contest and was awarded a recording contract with Pye records. With no backing group to assist in the recording of his first single, Little called in The Checkmates to help out, although the result, "I Understand Just How You Feel" was credited to Jimmy Justice – his new stage name – and The Jury and released in 1960.

The single failed to make an impact in the UK charts, as did his second release, "When Love Has Left You" and, somewhat disillusioned, Justice moved to Sweden to be with his Swedish girlfriend. He then divided his time between the recording studios in England, where he worked with the producer Tony Hatch, and working in clubs in Sweden, where he had gained exposure on radio and TV.

Jimmy Justice had a singing style which closely resembled the black American soul singers and his third release was a double cover of the American doo wop group The Jarmels record "Little Lonely One" backed with "A Little Bit Of Soap". This again failed to appear in the UK charts, but the A side was however a greater success in Sweden.

In 1962, Jimmy Justice attained the peak of his UK success, when he recorded three songs destined to reach the top 20. In March that year he released his cover version of the American group The Drifters' song "When My Little Girl Is Smiling" and despite competition from both the original and another cover version by Craig Douglas, his version reached a creditable number 9 in the UK charts in March.

Justice diverted from cover versions of American records for his next release, by choosing a song composed by Les Vandyke, who was then working closely with Eden Kane. The song, "Ain't That Funny" turned out to be Justice's greatest hit when it peaked at number 8 in the UK charts in June.

Despite his success with the Les Vandyke song, Justice returned to the American songbook for his final chart success, a cover version of "Spanish Harlem", which just reached the top 20 in August. The song led to Jimmy Justice being known as Britain's Ben E. King, but sadly he was unable to capitalize on his previous successes and his career faded, along with many others, with the imminent arrival of the beat boom.

1962 was something of a transition year in British popular music. It was an eclectic mix of music, with stalwarts from the heady days of British rock 'n' roll such as Cliff Richard and Billy Fury continuing to enjoy chart success – even the skiffle aficionados could be satisfied with Lonnie Donegan's "Pick A Bale Of Cotton" in August, 1962 – mixed in with the newer easy listening styles of Mark Wynter and Jimmy Justice.

However, just as in the previous decade, there was room in the charts in the early 1960's for unusual styles and 'oddities'.

With a combination of easy listening and a throw back to the cowboy singing styles of a previous era, the English born, Australian raised Frank Ifield surprised most people when his yodelling song, "I Remember You" raced up the charts to the number 1 position in July, 1962, followed in October when "Lovesick Blues" – again complete with yodel – gave him his second UK chart topper for the year.

Frank Ifield had previously established himself as an entertainer in Australia and at the age of just 19 was regarded as the number one recording star, but in 1959 returned to the land he had left in 1946 to try his luck.

Based on his Australian career, Ifield won a recording contract with EMI and was soon in the studios with the producer Norrie Paramor. His first record, released in 1960, was "Lucky Devil" and reached number 22 in the UK charts. However, Ifield could be excused for thinking himself anything but lucky, as his next six releases failed to enter the top thirty, with only one record, the 1960 "Gotta Get A Date" charting at a lowly number 48.

With his confidence low, Ifield then recorded "I Remember You", which proved to be the start of a successful string of top thirty charting records up until 1966, including the number 1 hits "Wayward Wind" and "Confessin'" in 1963.

Another who scored success with a yodelling style was the Glaswegian Angus Murdo McKenzie. Starting his working life in the Norwegian merchant navy at just 15, after five years McKenzie left the navy to join the Argyll and Southern Highland Regiment.

During his army service he was in action in the Korean War, but after his discharge he rejoined the merchant navy and travelled the world before jumping ship in America and settling in Nashville for a while, where he developed his western cowboy singing style – and changed his name to Karl Denver.

Unfortunately he was deported from America in 1959, when he was discovered to be an illegal immigrant, and returned to Britain, where he based himself in Manchester. He formed the Karl Denver Trio with Kevin Neil and Gerry Cottrell and soon caught the attention of the TV producer Jack Good, who featured the trio on his TV programme *Wham!* and managed to gain them a place on a national UK tour headlined by Billy Fury and featuring Jess Conrad.

The TV appearances resulted in a recording contract with Decca records and the trio had immediate success with their first two records, "Marcheta" and "Mexacali Rose", which both reached number 8 in the UK charts in June and October, 1961 respectively.

The Karl Denver Trio's third release became their greatest chart success, however, with a re-working of the song, eventually credited to a Zulu tribesman named Solomon Linda, entitled "Wimoweh".

Despite the song – under the alternative title "The Lion Sleeps Tonight" – having had chart success with both The Tokens and The Weavers in America, the Karl Denver Trio version reached a very creditable number 4 in the UK charts in January, 1962.

Further hits followed during 1962, but chart placings became harder to come by and 1963 saw only one top 20 record, the song

"Still" – backed by the oddly named "My Canary Has Circles Under His Eyes" – which peaked at number 13.

Karl Denver's hit parade days may have been over, but he continued to enjoy success as a live act in cabaret in Scotland and the north of England during the next few years. His career was briefly rekindled in 1989 when he collaborated with the Manchester band The Happy Mondays to record "Lazyitis (One Armed Boxer)" which reached number 46 in the UK charts.

So, with yodelling, ballads, a bit of Trad Jazz and the occasional up-tempo record from the likes of the American group B. Bumble and The Stingers – who reached number 1 with their "Nut Rocker" in May, 1962, the UK charts certainly presented a cosmopolitan look in 1962.

The year was also the time that dance crazes took hold in the UK, with American artists such as Chubby Checker, Joey Dee and The Starlighters, Sam Cooke and even Frank Sinatra pushing the Twist and Little Eva with the Locomotion. Surprisingly enough, the only British artist to have chart success with a Twist song was the perennial Petula Clark, with her "Ya Ya Twist" in July, 1962.

It seemed that just about the only genre unrepresented in the UK charts was the comedy record, but this was soon remedied by two unlikely acts, Bernard Cribbins and Mike Sarne.

After serving an apprenticeship in the Oldham Repertory Theater – interrupted by his national service in the parachute regiment of the British army – Bernard Cribbins soon found employment in the West End theater scene, taking roles in *Not Now Darling* and *Run For Your Wife* among others.

He also gained success in his film career, appearing in films such as *Dunkirk*, *Make Mine A Million* and *Two Way Stretch* in 1959.

He also found time to perform in a revue called *...And Another Thing*, written by musician Ted Dicks and lyricist Myles Rudge. During his performance, Cribbins was called upon to sing a satirical song called "Folk Song"

The song caught the attention of EMI producer George Martin, who at the time was specializing in novelty records with Parlophone records and Cribbins recorded the song in 1960 under Martin's production. Sadly, it failed to make any impact on the charts.

However, in 1962 Cribbins was again back in the studios with George Martin, with two songs by the Dicks/Rudge combination. The first of these "Hole In The Ground" – concerning an exasperated council road worker who gains the ultimate revenge on a toffee nosed bystander – tickled the fancy of the record buying public and the record reached number 9 in the UK charts in March, 1962.

The second song, "Right, Said Fred" – concerning the exploits of three workmen attempting to move a grand piano – also scored chart success and reached number 10 in the UK charts in July the same year.

A third song, also recorded under the auspices of George Martin, but written by Trevor Peacock, called "Gypsy Calypso" reached number 25 in the UK charts later in 1962, but proved to be the final chart success for this unlikely pop singer.

Cribbins did however go on to have much greater success on TV – where he was the narrator for the children's series *The Wombles* and appeared in the *Dr. Who* series – and in his film career where he was a regular in the *Carry On* series of British comedy films.

The other unlikely act to score success with comedy in the UK charts during 1962 was the Czechoslovakian born Michael Scheuer, who later adopted the stage name Mike Sarne.

After leaving school, Sarne, who had an ear for languages, enrolled in the School of Slavonic and East European Studies – part of University College, London – to study for a BA in languages.

His language skills brought him into contact with Robert Stigwood and Joe Meek, who employed him to provide phonetic voice guidance tracks for artists such as John Leyton when they re-recorded their songs in a foreign language for the European market.

Mike Sarne could also play guitar and sing and was signed as a recording artist in his own right by Stigwood and, with the help of Joe Meek and a young actress, Wendy Richard[10], recorded the novelty song "Come Outside".

Once again, the comedy aspects of the attempts by a boy (Mike Sarne) to persuade his girlfriend (Wendy Richard) to accompany him outside the dance hall proved popular with the record buying public, and the record reached number 1 in the UK charts in May, 1962.

The follow up record, "Will I What?" followed a similar format, with the girl this time portrayed by a young female singer Billie Davis, who would later have her own hit record with a cover of The Exciters "Tell Him". The novelty had perhaps begun to wane by this time, and the record struggled to reach number 18 in the UK charts in August, 1962.

Subsequent singles, "Just For Kicks" and "Code Of Love" barely scratched the lower reaches of the hit parade and Mike Sarne's recording career was over by the end of 1964. He did however go on to have a successful career as writer, actor and movie director, with his biggest success being the director of the film *Myra Breckinridge* which starred Raquel Welch, Mae West and Farrah Fawcett in her first film role.

Perhaps symptomatic of the middle of the road lethargy which had overtaken British popular music by 1962 was the close harmony style and all-round 'niceness' of the Irish singing group The Bachelors.

The Bachelors – the two brothers Conleth and Declan Clusky, together with friend John Stokes, started their show business life in 1957 as a classically styled harmonica playing group they called The Harmonichords, or sometimes The Harmony Chords.

The boys appeared on the radio talent show *Opportunity Knocks*, hosted on Radio Luxembourg by popular personality Hughie Green and even made an appearance on America's The Ed Sullivan Show, when a St. Patrick's Day special was broadcast from Dublin on March 15, 1959.

After incorporating singing into their act and turning more towards folk singing, the trio were signed by Decca records A&R manager Dick Rowe, who considered them sufficiently different from the current blend of pop music to be worthy of a recording contract – an opinion he would not apply to The Beatles later in his career.

At Rowe's suggestion, The Harmonichords changed their name to the more appealing – to teenage girls perhaps – The Bachelors, although all the boys were by now married.

The group's first single release for Decca was a re-working of the old favourite "Charmaine" – a hit for Mantovani and His Orchestra way back in 1951 – and The Bachelors lilting Irish accents lifted the record to number 6 in January, 1963.

1963 also saw chart success with firstly "Faraway Places" and then "Whispering" before the boys struck their first number 1 in January, 1961 with "Diane".

Even though by now the Mersey sound was sweeping the country, The Bachelors scored four further top ten hits during the remainder of 1963 and 1964, but their last significant charting was with the Paul Simon song "The Sound Of Silence" which reached number 3 in the UK charts in March, 1966.

So by the end of 1962 the charts were dominated by the smooth sounds that the record companies were comfortable with – the rawness, excitement and at times amateurism of the records of those six years between 1956 and 1962 had been sandpapered down to a sanitized blandness.

But the younger generation, unencumbered by the responsibilities of parenthood, rent payments and the cost of living, still had a spark smouldering, a remnant of the time when rock 'n' roll was king.

Driven by a desire to recover those times, they started to go back to the originators of rock 'n' roll, to see where the inspiration had come from – and perhaps recreate it.

All over the country, in homes, small clubs and even in garages, youngsters could be heard exploring the music of the almost unheard of originators of rhythm and blues music. Musicians like Muddy Waters, Memphis Slim, Elmore James and Robert Johnson would prove the inspiration for the next great – and I truly mean great – tidal wave of British popular music that would flood all over the world.

Chapter Eleven: – Whatever Happened To?

"What're You Going To Do When It's All Over?"
(Al Stewart – Class of '58)

Of all the thousands of would-be stars who picked up a guitar, a washboard, or made themselves a broomstick bass in the late 1950's, only a small percentage enjoyed success – and of those relative few the majority slipped from the public eye as quickly as melting snow.

For many, their few moments in the limelight are only memories from a time when they were the idols of thousands across the country, forgotten now by all but a few.

Even from the early days of rock 'n' roll the common question asked of the latest hit parade conqueror was 'what will you do when you no longer have hits?' Nobody expected a long term career from the music business – certainly not from rock 'n' roll – and the idea of still performing after reaching retirement age seemed a very unlikely proposition.

Many, unfortunately, are no longer alive as illness and plain old age have claimed them. Some live on in relative obscurity, while others still perform on the 'golden oldies' circuits and relive their successes to an audience of nostalgic fans eager to recapture their own youth.

There are some of those early performers, however, who have continued to be successful by changing their acts, appealing to different audiences or changing their careers from singing stars to production roles or TV and film acting.

It would take another book to record the details of the events in the lives of all the performers mentioned in this book, so I'll limit myself to a brief run-down of the later careers of the major players of the forgotten years.

The first British teen idol was of course Tommy Steele, and he managed to turn his rock 'n' roll career into that of a very successful family entertainer. From his early beginnings it was clear that his success was based more on his personality and charisma rather than sex appeal, and it was no surprise when he developed his performances towards a wider audience.

After his initial success as a rock 'n' roll singer, Tommy Steele expanded his career firstly through film appearances in movies such as *The Duke Wore Jeans* and *Tommy The Toreador* before moving into musical theater, where he achieved great success with stage appearances in *Half A Sixpence* in both London's West End and on Broadway.

He holds the record for the artist who has headlined the most ever performances at the London Palladium and has regularly appeared there in the role of Scrooge in the production of *Scrooge The Musical* based on Charles Dicken's *A Christmas Carol*.

As recently as November, 2013, Tommy Steele is set to tour the UK with a production of this musical stage show.

The perpetually youthful looking Cliff Richard also managed to extend his career through several decades, initially through films in the Elvis Presley mould, such as *The Young Ones* and *Summer Holiday* but has mainly presented himself as an all-round family entertainer rather than venturing into serious film or stage roles.

From his first record, "Move It", Cliff Richard has seen his career span more than 50 years and has been honoured with several gold and platinum records, three 'Brit' awards and two 'Ivor Novello' awards. He has the distinction of having had a number 1 UK chart record in every decade between the 1950's and the 1990's and in November, 2013 he released his 100th album, *The Fabulous Rock 'N' Roll Songbook*.

In December, 2009 Cliff Richard and The Shadows celebrated 50 years in the music business with the 'Golden Anniversary Concert Tour of the UK' which was extended into Europe during the beginning of 2010.

Despite his immense popularity in the UK, Europe and Australasia, Cliff Richard failed to make a similar impact in America, although he can boast eight singles entries in the Billboard charts over the 1950's, 1960's, 1970's and 1980's.

For a teenage idol, marriage can be a death knell for a career, as Marty Wilde found out to his cost when he married the ex-Vernons Girl Joyce Baker in 1959. Riding high with his appearances on *Oh Boy!* and *Boy Meets Girls*, Marty Wilde's career took a nosedive after his marriage became known.

Although he attempted to resurrect his career by forming a trio with his wife and Justin Hayward – later to become famous as a member of The Moody Blues – the trio, known as The Wilde Three – had limited success.

Wilde however achieved success as a songwriter, teaming with Ronnie Scott – not to be confused with the jazz club owner of the same name – in writing the song "Jesamine" for the one-hit wonders The Casuals, "I'm A Tiger" for Lulu and "Ice In The Sun" for Status Quo, all under the pseudonyms of Frere Manston and Jack Gellar.

Marty Wilde did have one final chart record, when the Manston/Gellar composition "Abergavenny", recorded under the artistic name of Shannon, reached number 47 in the UK charts, but he is now probably best remembered as the father of 1980's rock star Kim Wilde, who scored a big hit with "Kids In America", co written by Marty and his son Ricky Wilde. Ricky, after a short career as a pop singer, has gone on to become a successful record producer and composer.

With a UK tour underway at the time of writing in 2013, Marty Wilde can still attract audiences who fondly remember him. Indeed, his latest CD, *Born To Rock 'N' Roll – The Greatest Hits* is a true celebration of his fifty years in the recording business.

Apart from Tommy Steele, Cliff Richard and Marty Wilde, the other best remembered artist from those exciting days of rock 'n' roll is Billy Fury.

Billy Fury suffered from heart problems as a result of his child-hood illness, rheumatic fever, and in 1970, and again in 1971 he underwent heart surgery. He recovered from these setbacks and had a starring role in the movie *That'll Be The Day* which also featured David Essex and Ringo Starr.

However, his heart problems re-emerged in 1976 and he was again forced to undergo heart surgery, following which he slipped from the public gaze into semi retirement on his 100 acre farm near Llandovery in Wales.

Billy Fury was declared bankrupt in 1978, a situation for which he blamed Larry Parnes, claiming that Parnes had paid his wages, but had neglected to pay his tax liabilities. He tried to remedy the situation by re-recording several of his biggest hits for the budget record label K-Tel and was eventually discharged from his bankruptcy a year later.

In the early 1980's Billy Fury once again began recording, work-ing on a new album *The One And Only Billy Fury* but before this could be released, he suffered a collapse at his farm on March 7, 1982 and was once more hospitalized. After making a seemingly good re-covery and with a TV appearance and national tour, the future was once again looking bright, but on January 28, 1983, Billy Fury was discovered unconscious in his London flat and despite being rushed to hospital, he died the same day, aged just 42 years old.

After his initial success on the TV show *Six-Five Special*, Terry Dene appeared to be on the road to stardom, but a series of incidents, culminating in his arrest for drunkenness and then his discharge only a short time after his call up for national service, effectively put a stop to his promising recording career.

Disillusioned by his treatment by the press, in 1964 Terry Dene turned to religion and turned his singing and composing talents towards a series of religious records. He toured the continent as a preacher and performed in churches and prisons, in particular in Scandinavia, where he married for a second time.

In 1974 Terry Dene released a book and accompanying album, contemplatively called *I Thought Terry Dene Was Dead* and began performing with his group The Dene Aces, which included the bass player Brian Gregg, late of Johnny Kid and The Pirates.

A compilation of the best of his recordings for Decca was released in December, 2004 on the Vocalion record label and in December, 2012, under his own recording company, Terry Dene released *The Best Of Terry Dene*, a selection of 12 tracks including a new recording of his own song "Com'in And Be Loved".

Like Tommy Steele, another of the so-called Elvis clones was Adam Faith and like Tommy, Adam Faith moved away from rock 'n' roll at quite an early stage in his career. With the advent of the Mersey beat boom in the early part of the 1960's, Adam Faith had his final UK top ten chart hit in October 1963, with "The First Time".

His career took a change of direction after that, as he gradual moved away from singing and – perhaps surprisingly to some – into repertory theater, where he played several small roles before landing the lead role in the touring stage production of *Billy Liar.*

By 1970 Adam Faith had married – to dancer Jackie Irving – and had moved into the music management business – among his protégées was Leo Sayer – and had gained the starring role in the TV series *Budgie,* about an ex-convict.

He returned to film work in 1975, beginning with a role in the movie *Stardust*, which starred David Essex and Ringo Starr, and followed by a supporting role in the movie *McVicar*, which featured The Who's lead singer Roger Daltrey in the lead role.

In the 1980's, Adam Faith turned his hand to investments and wrote a financial column in the Daily Mail and Sunday Mail newspapers, together with co-hosting a TV show *The Money Channel* with Paul Killik. However, when the show closed in 1982, it was revealed that Adam Faith had made considerable investment losses, not only for himself but also for others following his investment advice, and he was declared bankrupt in June, 1982, owing a reported £32 million.

Adam Faith underwent open heart surgery in 1986 but recovering from these setbacks, he starred in the TV series *Love Hurts* with actress Zoë Wannamaker between 1992 and 1994, before returning to theater work in several productions of the stage play *Alfie*.

He had come offstage after appearing in a touring production of the play *Love And Marriage* in Stoke-on-Trent on March 7, 2003 when he became ill and was taken to hospital, where he died early the next morning from a heart attack, aged just 62.

But what of those other stars from the Larry Parnes stable? With a successful expansion of Tommy Steele's career into a fully fledged all-round family entertainer, and Billy Fury's status as a top attraction as both a strong balladeer and straight out rock 'n' roller, Parnes was keen for his other 'boys' to make the step up from being purely rock 'n' roll singers.

Unfortunately for Parnes, many of his artists were unable to make that transition and faded from the music scene as quickly as they had appeared. Johnny Gentle, for example whose main claim to fame may well be the fact that he had The Beatles as his backing group for a short time on a tour of Scotland, changed his name to Darren Young in 1962, but his only record under this name, "I've Just Fallen For Someone", failed to make any impact.

In 1964 he replaced Gordon Mills – later composer of the Tom Jones hit "It's Not Unusual" – in another of Larry Parnes' groups, The

Viscounts, but shortly after the group broke up. Johnny Gentle then retired from the music business to become a joiner in Jersey before moving to Kent, where in 1998 he published a book reminiscing of his tour with The Beatles, titled *Johnny Gentle And The Beatles: First Ever Tour.*

Vince Eager can justifiably account for his demise from rock stardom with his split from Larry Parnes in 1960, following the publicity Parnes attempted to gain from the death in a car accident of Eager's friend and fellow rocker Eddie Cochran.

Following his split from Parnes, Vince Eager spent much of his time touring the club circuit and in pantomime before scoring the lead role in the West End stage musical *Elvis*, directed by Jack Good and in which he starred for five years. Other rock 'n' roll luminaries to appear over the life of the long running show included P.J. Proby and Shakin' Stevens.

In 1986 Vince Eager had a complete career change when he moved to Fort Lauderdale, Texas and took up the position as a cruise director on American luxury cruise liners, but the lure of England was too strong and he returned to England, where he now lives with his wife Anette and close to his two sons and their families.

Vince Eager has since published his memoirs in the book *Vince Eager's Rock 'n' Roll Files* and in 2007, Pink 'n' Black records released all his early singles on a 2-CD compilation called *The Complete Vince Eager.*

Unfortunately several of the Larry Parnes family were unable to cope with the pressures involved with rock 'n' roll performances. Dickie Pride was one of those who failed to make the transition from rock 'n' roll to family entertainer and after an unsuccessful release of an album of standards, backed by The Eric Jupp Orchestra entitled *Pride Without Prejudice*, which failed miserably, he was dropped from the Parnes entourage.

Dickie Pride was by then suffering from mental health and drug related problems and in 1967 he was admitted to a psychiatric hospital, where he underwent a lobotomy. Sadly, Dickie Pride – considered by both Billy Fury and Joe Brown as one of the best singers of his era – died from an overdose of sleeping pills on March 26, 1969, aged just 27 years old.

Another who suffered from the stresses and temptations of the rock 'n' roll life style was Britain's equivalent of Gene Vincent, Vince Taylor. Although many people on first meeting him thought he was American, Vince Taylor was in fact born in England, but spent his youth and teenage years in America before returning to Britain and forging his career as a rock 'n' roller with his group The Playboys.

With black leather stage gear and stage antics and posturing very similar to Gene Vincent, Vince Taylor was considered the wild man of British rock 'n' roll. However, after his encounter with LSD and the acid rock scene in London during a trip there from Paris, Vince Taylor was never the same again, claiming to be the prophet Mathew, the son of Jesus Christ.

At the time David Bowie remarked that he wasn't sure if he thought Taylor was an alien or the son of God – perhaps a bit of both – but Bowie certainly based his latter creation Ziggy Stardust very much on Vince Taylor's persona.

After a few abortive performances during which Taylor attempted to preach to his audiences and even anoint them from a water jug, he soon disappeared from the public eye. He reappeared briefly at the end of the 1960's, following a campaign by two French musical newspapers, Disco Revue and Bonjour Les Amis, to have the iconic rock singer return to the stage and indeed he did make intermittent appearances during the 1970's.

Vince Taylor ended his days working as an aircraft mechanic in Lausanne, Switzerland, where he died on August 28, 1991 and the relatively young age of 52.

Having had the name Lance Fortune bestowed on him by Larry Parnes, Chris Morris may have hoped for better things after scoring chart success with two of his first four records, but unfortunately this was not meant to be. Despite being called up, along with the American Jerry Keller, as late replacements for the ill-fated Gene Vincent/Eddie Cochran tour following Cochran's death in a road accident, Lance Fortune's recording career failed to provide any further hits.

With no further success as a solo performer forthcoming, Lance Fortune joined forces with his backing group of the time, The Staggerlees, playing bass and singing but from there he seems to have disappeared without trace, although rumour has it that he is still alive and living 'somewhere up north'.

Having missed out on the name Lance Fortune, the newly christened Georgie Fame achieved considerable success with his group The Blue Flames in the mid 1960's before splitting and working as a solo act.

In the 1970's Georgie Fame collaborated with Alan Price – ex keyboard player in The Animals – to produce the hit record "Rosetta" in 1971 but in 1974 he reformed The Blue Flames and worked with a number of big bands and leading orchestras.

Georgie Fame has worked with some of the biggest names in the music industry, including Van Morrison, Count Basie and Eric Clapton and was a founding member of Bill Wyman's Rhythm Kings. He formed his own record label – Three Line Whip – in the late 1990's and has released several albums of his own jazz and rhythm and blues compositions.

After his success in the West End musical *Charley Girl* in the late 1960's and with three seasons of his own ITV television programme *The Joe Brown Show* behind him, in the 1970's Joe Brown formed a new group, which he named Brown's Home Brew, together with his old friend Pete Oakman from The Bruvvers. The band played a musical collection of Brown's own hits together with gospel and country songs and had some success.

Joe Brown became good friends with The Beatles' George Harrison – Harrison was best man at Joe Brown's second marriage in 2000 and The Beatles were the support act for Joe Brown before they hit the big time – and the two musicians shared a love of the ukulele; so much so that Joe Brown performed a moving tribute to Harrison by playing the old standard "I'll See You In My Dreams" accompanying himself on the ukulele as a memorable finale to the tribute concert to Harrison after the latter's death from lung cancer on November 29, 2001.

In 2008 Joe Brown celebrated 50 years in the music business by accepting a gold disc for his compilation album *Joe Brown – The Very Best Of* and completing a gruelling 37 week tour in the Spring and a 36 week tour in the Autumn, interspersed with a sell-out concert at the Royal Albert Hall which included Mark Knopler, Dave Edmunds and his daughter from his first marriage, Sam Brown.

At the time of writing (November 2013) Joe Brown continues to pull in audiences as he tours Britain yet again and has just released his latest album *The Ukulele Album*.

Many of the lesser stars from the late 1950's and early 1960's were unable to take advantage of their moments of fame and sank back into oblivion very quickly, as we have seen. One who did develop his talents within the music industry – although not directly as a stage performer – was Emile Ford.

Emile Ford achieved success with his group The Checkmates at the end of the 1950's with the number 1 chart listing "What Do You Want To Make Those Eyes At Me For". He was always keenly interested in the quality of the audio aspects of his performances, admitting that he had a poor voice and using his technical knowledge to produce a superior sound quality.

As early as 1960, Emile Ford had developed his own system for backing tracks for use on stage – perhaps the world's first karaoke system – and by 1969 he had set up his own recording studio in Barbados.

He moved to Scandinavia early in the 1970's, where he further developed his playback systems, before moving to California – possibly to escape the cold Scandinavian winters – where he has established his own company, Sound Revelation Services, with affiliates in Stockholm (The Art Of Mastering), St. Lucia (E.F. Sound St. Lucia Sound) and Britain (E.F. Quantum Sound P-Mastering.

Although Wee Willie Harris all but vanished from the music scene after his initial successes at the end of the 1950's, he did gain some publicity in the late 1970's, when he gained an honourable mention in the Ian Drury record "Reasons To Be Cheerful, Part 3". Harris responded somewhat belatedly in 2000 with a new album of his own entitled *Twenty Reasons To Be Cheerful*.

As recently as November, 2013, a twitter campaign – apparently unsuccessful – was started to try to get the Wee Willie Harris version of "Got A Match" into the UK charts, something he had been unable to do during his solo career.

After the success of the single "I'll Never Get Over You" at the beginning of the Merseybeat Boom, Johnny Kidd And The Pirates struggled to find further success. In 1964 guitarist Mick Green became increasingly dispirited and left to join Billy J Kramer's backing group, The Dakotas, to be replaced firstly by John Weider, who had played with The Tony Meehan Combo and also with Steve Marriot of The Small Faces, and then when Weider left in September, 1965, by Jon Morshead.

By April 1966 Johnny Kidd had married his long term girlfriend, Jean Complin, but the lack of record successes eventually forced a break-up between Kidd And The Pirates. Having blessed the breakaway band with the name, Johnny Kidd had intended to go for a solo career, but soon realized that he needed a backing group for his stage and recording commitments and recruited a new group from the remnants of the backing group for Buddy Britten, namely The Regents.

Unwilling to give up totally on his stage persona, the new combination was launched as Johnny Kidd And The New Pirates and initially consisted of organist Ray Soaper, drummer Roger Pinner, bassist Nick Simper and guitarist Mick Stewart. However, after Soaper missed a gig in Somerset as a result of a last minute change of plans, the group decided that the simple power trio of guitar, bass and drums sounded more effective, and Soaper was asked to leave.

Things began to look up again, but sadly the good fortune was short-lived. Late on the evening of October 7, 1966, the car in which Johnny Kidd was a passenger was involved in a head-on crash near Bury, Lancashire. Despite the efforts of firemen and ambulance personnel, Johnny Kidd was pronounced dead on arrival at Bolton Royal Infirmary. The final record featuring Johnny Kidd and The New Pirates, "Send For That Girl" was released in November 1966, but unlike other posthumous releases by other singers, was not a great success.

The other notable performer with a theatrical stage performance, Screaming Lord Sutch, although not as successful record-wise as Johnny Kidd, did have a somewhat longer, albeit varied career.

In 1964, picking up on the popularity of pirate radio stations off the coast of England broadcasting pop music in direct competition with the BBC, Sutch and his manager Reginald Calvert took over an anti-aircraft defence fort complex, known as Shivering Sands, used during World War Two and set up the pirate radio station Radio Sutch.

Sutch's involvement was short-lived, however, and the station soon changed its name to Radio City, under which name it continued to broadcast until 1967, when government legislation forced the closure of pirate radio stations – and a radical re-shaping of the BBC radio programming.

A short residence in America followed, but after being the subject of a mugging attempt there, David Sutch returned to England in the early 1980's, where he resurrected his colourful but unsuccessful political career, which had started from his unsuccessful by-election in 1963 as a candidate for the National Teenage Party.

In 1983 he formed the Official Monster Raving Loony Party, and for which he stood as a candidate at the Bermondsey by-election in the same year. He continued his political career up until November, 1997, with his final political appearance being the Winchester by-election at which he recorded just 316 votes, or 0.6% of the total.

Sadly, David Sutch suffered from depression and, following the death of his mother in 1998, he hanged himself on June 16, 1999.

Although he himself recognised that he did not have a very good voice, David Sutch managed to surround himself with excellent fellow musicians and worked with, apart from those already mentioned in Chapter Four, such luminaries as Keith Moon, Jimmy Page, Jeff Beck and Charlie Watts.

Our local heroes, The Wild Oats? Yes, like many others from the era they faded away, but in 1995 a recording – made by dedicated fans on a reel-to-reel tape recorder – of their live performance at the International Club in their home town of Leiston, Suffolk in May 1964 was released on the Tenth Planet record label, entitled *The Wild Oats – Live At Leiston* in a limited edition of 500. I am the proud owner of limited edition number 324.

Epilogue: – The Curtain Falls On Act One

"One day they'll make TV shows on ageing rock 'n' rollers"
(Al Stewart – Class of '58)

During the years between 1956 and 1962 life in Britain changed in ways not seen before. Teenagers became the dominant spending force in the music retail business, 78 rpm shellac records gave way to 45 rpm vinyl records and TV and radio programming followed the switch to a youth orientated society.

The austerity years immediately after the war gave way to a period of relatively more prosperity. Across the country tens of thousands of teenagers were captured by the immediacy and simplicity of skiffle music and tempted to try it for themselves.

Of those tens of thousands, a few found themselves in the right place at the right time and found fame and fortune beyond their wildest dreams. For some, the success became a burden too great to bear and they succumbed to the old adage of 'sex, drugs and rock 'n' roll' while others, after their initial success, adapted their performances to attract wider audiences and were able to continue their careers – some are still going strong today.

But of all the things that music had going for it during those few short years, it must be the fun and excitement that is remembered most fondly. As Lonnie Donegan said when interviewed by Michael Aspel on the TV show *The Trouble With The Fifties* back in the 1990's – 'The key word is fun. It was a totally different world back then than it is today. In those days, the kids had fun. You didn't go out to make a million, you did it for fun.'

And indeed that was the case. The music had a joyousness about it and if was only three chords, who cared? The over complications, the layered levels of sound would come, certainly, but in the beginning, the music was, as Al Stewart so aptly put it, 'the sound of being young'.

Today the importance of those early days, so often forgotten, is finally being recognized. The breakthroughs and impacts made by those original British skiffle players and rock 'n' rollers in changing the way music was appreciated and indeed the way the whole music business operated is acknowledged as laying the foundations for the next great change in musical society.

Join me after the interval as the curtain rises on act two – the coming of the Beat Boom...

Appendix 1- Significant Events 1956

January	Bill Haley reaches number 1 in the UK charts with "Rock Around The Clock". Petula Clark begins TV series on BBC TV.
February	Dean Martin at number 1 with "Memories Are Made Of This". Associated Television (ATV) begins TV broadcasts in the Midlands on weekdays only.
March	Winifred Atwell at number 1 with "The Poor People Of Paris". Pakistan declares itself the first Islamic Republic.
April	Winifred Atwell still at number 1 with "The Poor People Of Paris". Russia announces it has the capability to launch intercontinental ballistic missiles loaded with hydrogen bombs. Ampex demonstrates first commercial video recorder.
May	Ronnie Hilton reaches number 1 with "No Other Love". Granada TV begins broadcasting in northern England on weekdays only
June	Pat Boone at number 1 with "I'll Be Home". The Goons reach number 4 with "I'm Walking Backwards For Christmas"
July	The Teenagers with Frankie Lymon at number 1 with "Why Do Fools Fall In Love". President Nasser claims the Suez Canal.
August	Doris Day at number 1 with "Whatever Will Be Will Be". Tony Crombie and The Rockets formed.
September	Anne Shelton at number 1 with "Lay Down Your Arms". Tommy Steele and The Steelmen record "Rock With The Caveman" in London.
October	Frankie Laine at number 1 with "A Woman In Love". Tony Crombie and The Rockets enter the charts at number 25 with "(We're Gonna) Teach You To Rock". Tommy Steele and The Steelmen enter the charts with "Rock With The Caveman".
November	Johnny Ray at number 1 with "Just Walkin' In The Rain". President Eisenhower re-elected for a second term in America.
December	Tommy Steele and The Steelmen at number 1 with "Singing The Blues". Little Richard enters the UK charts at number 30 with "Rip It Up".

Appendix 2- Significant Events 1957

January	Tommy Steele and The Steelmen and Guy Mitchell swap the number 1 position with "Singing The Blues". Harold Macmillan becomes UK Prime Minister after the resignation of Anthony Eden.
February	Tab Hunter number 1 with "Young Love". The *Six-Five Special* premiers on BBC TV
March	Tab Hunter still number 1 in the UK charts. Bill Haley and His Comets perform at the Regal Theater, Edmonton. European Economic Community formed with the signing of the Treaty of Rome.
April	Lonnie Donegan takes over at number 1 with "Cumberland Gap". British Government introduces legislation aimed at ending national service after 1960
May	Andy Williams at number 1 with "Butterfly" Ronnie Hilton, Bing Crosby, Mantovani and Gracie Fields all in the UK charts with "Around The World".
June	Lonnie Donegan at number 1 with "Putting On The Style". Joe Meek sets up his first recording studio in an apartment in Arundell Road, Portobello Markets.
July	Elvis Presley at number 1 with "All Shook Up". Tony Crombie breaks up The Rockets. Althea Gibson becomes first black female player to win at Wimbledon tennis championships.
August	Paul Anka at number 1 with "Diana". Tony Crombie breaks up The Rockets.
September	Paul Anka continues at number 1 with "Diana". Westrex demonstrate stereo discs in America. America conducts first underground nuclear test in the Nevada desert.
October	Paul Anka continues at number 1 with "Diana". Russia launches first satellite, Sputnik, into orbit
November	The Crickets at number 1 with "That'll Be The Day" Outside broadcast of The *Six-Five Special* from the 2 I's coffee bar.
December	Harry Belafonte at number 1 with "Mary's Boy Child"

Appendix 3- Significant Events 1958

January	Jerry Lee Lewis at number 1 with "Great Balls Of Fire" followed by Elvis Presley with "Jailhouse Rock". America launches the Explorer satellite from Cape Canaveral, Florida.
February	Perry Como at number 1 with "Magic Moments". Plane carrying Manchester United football team crashes on takeoff at Munich airport, killing seven members of the team.
March	Perry Como remains at number 1. Elvis Presley starts national service in the American army. The Westrex stereo recording system adopted as the industry standard.
April	Marvin Rainwater at number 1 with "Whole Lotta Woman". Tommy Steele injured by fans at a concert in Glasgow after a security failure. Cliff Richard changes his name from Harry Webb.
May	Connie Francis at number 1 with "Who's Sorry Now". Lonnie Donegan record "Nobody Loves Like An Irishman" banned by the BBC.
June	Vic Damone at number 1 with "On The Street Where You Live". BBC premieres TV show *Juke Box Jury*.
July	The Everly Brothers at number 1 with "All I Have To Do Is Dream". Prince Charles named Price of Wales.
August	The Kalin Twins at number 1 with "When". Russia successfully launches and retrieves two dogs from space.
September	Connie Francis at number 1 with "Stupid Cupid". TV show *Oh Boy!* first broadcast, with Cliff Richard and The Drifters, Cuddly Dudley, Marty Wilde and The John Barry Seven.
October	Connie Francis remains at number 1 with "Stupid Cupid". Marty Wilde quits *Oh Boy!* over dispute over top billing with Cliff Richard.
November	Lord Rockingham's XI at number 1 with "Hoots Mon". Emile Ford appears on *Oh Boy!*
December	Conway Twitty at number 1 with "It's Only Make Believe". Last edition of the *Six-Five Special* broadcast by the BBC.

Appendix 4- Significant Events 1959

January	Elvis Presley at number 1 with the double A sided "I Got Stung/One Night". Russia launches Luna 1 space craft.
February	Shirley Bassey at number 1 with "As I Love You". Buddy Holly, Ritchie Valens and J. P. Richardson killed in plane crash in Iowa.
March	Russ Conway at number 1 with "Side Saddle". The Barbie Doll premieres in America.
April	Buddy Holly at number 1 with "It Doesn't Matter Anymore". NASA selects the first seven American astronauts, to be known as the Mercury Seven.
May	Elvis Presley at number 1 with the double A sided "A Fool Such As I/ I Need Your Love Tonight". Lansdowne Recording Studios, designed by Joe Meek, opens in London.
June	Russ Conway at number 1 with "Roulette". Queen Elizabeth and American President Eisenhower officially open the St. Lawrence Seaway.
July	Cliff Richard and The Drifters at number 1 with "Living Doll". The Drifters change their name to The Shadows.
August	Cliff Richard remains at number 1 with "Living Doll". The launch of the first Mini, the car designed by Alec Issigonis.
September	Craig Douglas at number 1 with "Only Sixteen". TV show *Boy Meets Girls* premieres.
October	Cliff Richard and The Shadows at number 1 with "Travelin' Light". Conservative party retains government in the UK elections.
November	Cliff Richard remains at number 1 with "Travelin' Light". Film *Expresso Bongo* starring Cliff Richard premieres in London.
December	Adam Faith at number 1 with "What Do You Want". America launches and recovers a monkey from Earth orbit.

Appendix 5- Significant Events 1960

January	Adam Faith at number 1 with "Poor Me".
	Elvis Presley promoted to Sergeant in the US Army.
February	Anthony Newley at number 1 with "Why".
	Prince Andrew born.
March	Adam Faith's "Poor Me" replaced at number 1 firstly by Johnny Preston ("Running Bear") and then by Lonnie Donegan with "My Old Man's A Dustman".
	Elvis Presley honourably discharged from US Army.
April	Anthony Newley at number 1 with "Do You Mind".
	America launches the first weather satellite, *TIROS-1*
May	The Everly Brothers at number 1 with "Cathy's Clown"
	Princess Margaret marries Antony Armstrong-Jones.
June	Eddie Cochran at number 1 with "Three Steps To Heaven".
	New Zealand begins TV broadcasts in Auckland.
July	Jimmy Jones at number 1 with "Good Timin'", replaced by Cliff Richard and The Shadows with "Please Don't Tease".
	Francis Chichester arrives in New York after a record breaking solo crossing of the Atlantic in forty days.
August	Johnny Kidd And The Pirates at number 1 with "Shakin' All Over" .
	Russia launches and recovers the satellite *Sputnik 5*, containing two dogs, two rats and forty mice.
September	The Shadows at number 1 with "Apache".
	Joe Meek establishes RGM Studios at 304 Holloway Road, London.
October	Roy Orbison at number 1 with "Only The Lonely".
	The first successful UK kidney transplant takes place in Edinburgh.
November	Elvis Presley at number 1 with "It's Now Or Never".
	John F. Kennedy beats Richard Nixon in the US Presidential election.
December	Elvis Presley continues at number 1 with "It's Now Or Never". Replaced by Cliff Richard and The Shadows "I Love You".
	Premiere of TV show *Coronation Street*.

Appendix 6- Significant Events 1961

January	Elvis Presley at number 1 with "Are You Lonesome To-night". America sends a chimpanzee, 'Ham', into space aboard a Mercury space capsule.
February	Petula Clark at number 1 with "Sailor". The Beatles make their debut at Liverpool's Cavern Club.
March	Everly Brothers at number 1 with double A sided "Walk Right Back/Ebony Eyes". BBC bans Nero and The Gladiators version of "In The Hall Of The Mountain King".
April	Elvis Presley at number 1 with "Wooden Heart". Yuri Gagarin becomes the first human in space, orbiting the Earth in *Vostok-1*
May	The Temperance Seven at number 1 with "You're Driving Me Crazy". American Alan Shepard becomes the first American in space in a Mercury space capsule
June	Elvis Presley at number 1 with "Surrender". Russian ballet dancer Rudolf Nureyev defects in Paris while performing with the Kirov ballet company.
July	The Everly Brothers at number 1 with "Temptation". American Gus Grissom becomes the second American in space in a sub-orbital Mercury space flight.
August	Eden Kane at number 1 with "Well I Ask You" followed by Helen Shapiro with "You Don't Know". Russian Gherman Titov becomes the second human to orbit the Earth, remaining in space for two days.
September	John Leyton at number 1 with "Johnny Remember Me". The Organization for European Economic Cooperation (OEEC) is replaced by the Organization for Economic Co-operation and Development (OECD).
October	Helen Shapiro ("Walkin' Back To Happiness") replaces The Shadows ("Kon-Tiki") at number 1. The British satirical magazine *Private Eye* first appears.
November	Elvis Presley at number 1 with double A sided "His Latest Flame/Little Sister". The novel *Catch 22* by Joseph Heller is published.
December	Frankie Vaughan at number 1 with "Tower Of Strength" soon replaced by Danny Williams with "Moon River". Ireland's first national television service begins broadcasting.

Appendix 7- Significant Events 1962

January	Cliff Richard and The Shadows at number 1 with "The Young Ones". The Beatles audition for Decca Records.
February	Elvis Presley at number 1 with "Rock-A-Hula Baby/Can't Help Falling In Love". John Glenn becomes the first American to orbit the Earth in a four hour, fifty-five minute space flight.
March	The Shadows at number 1 with "Wonderful Land". Bob Dylan releases his first LP, the self-titled *Bob Dylan* in America.
April	The Shadows remain at number 1 with "Wonderful Land". The American Ranger-4 spacecraft crashes into the moon.
May	B. Bumble and The Stingers at number 1 with "Nut Rocker" replaced by Elvis Presley with "Good Luck Charm". Scott Carpenter becomes the second American to orbit the Earth.
June	Mike Sarne and Wendy Richard at number 1 with "Come Outside". Brazil wins the football world cup in Chile, beating Czechoslovakia in the final 3 – 1.
July	Frank Ifield at number 1 with "I Remember You". The World's first communications satellite *Telstar* is launched and relays the first live trans-Atlantic TV signal.
August	Frank Ifield continues at number 1 with "I Remember You". The Beatles fire drummer Pete Best; his replacement is ex-Rory Storm and The Hurricanes Ringo Starr.
September	Elvis Presley at number 1 with "She's Not You". The modern environmentalist movement begins with the publication of the Rachel Carson book *Silent Spring*.
October	The Tornados at number 1 with "Telstar". The Beatles release their first single "Love Me Do". The Cuba missile crisis unfolds.
November	Frank Ifield at number 1 with "Lovesick Blues". Russia agrees to dismantle missile bases in Cuba. Britain and France sign the agreement to build the *Concord* supersonic airliner.
December	Elvis Presley at number 1 with "Return To Sender". The American space probe *Mariner 2* flies past Venus, becoming the first space vehicle to transmit data from another planet.

Index

The index is organized alphabetically as normal. Artists are listed by their first name, so that Eden Kane, for example, appears under 'E'. Records are grouped together by title, with singles and LPs grouped separately.

Guitar manufacturers are grouped under 'G' – Guitars and amplifiers and drums are grouped under 'A' – Amplifiers and 'D' – Drums respectively.

Radio and TV programmes, channels, films and stage shows are also grouped separately for convenience.

The Forgotten Years 1956 - 1962

B

C

D

F

G

H

I

J

L

M

N

O

P

Q

R

The Forgotten Years 1956 - 1962

Index

S

Y

Z

Notes

[1] Originally written as a 13-minute homage to the early days of British rock 'n' roll, the song was rejected as "too long" and subsequently appeared on the album "A Beach Full of Shells" in a shortened version

[2] Developed to address the post-war housing shortage in Britain, 156,623 of these pre-fabricated buildings were completed between 1945 and 1951. Today a handful still survive, a testament to a form of emergency housing initially designed to have a life span of only 10 years.

[3] In his speech at Bedford in July, 1957, Macmillan also prophetically warned of the dangers of inflation.

[4] Jackie Brenston was a saxophonist in Ike Turner's Kings of Rhythm and sang the vocal on 'Rocket 88'. The song was based on a 1947 song 'Cadillac Boogie' by Jimmy Liggins and influenced by an instrumental called 'Rocket 88 Boogie Parts 1 and 2' by Pete Johnson recorded in 1949.

[5] Dan Burley started his working career as a journalist, before forming his group Dan Burley and His Skiffle Boys in 1948. Members of the group included the blues singer Brownie McGhee.

[6] Big Jim Sullivan was born James George Tompkins, but changed his name to Jimmy Sullivan, thinking it sounded more like Lonnie Donegan. He became a well-known session musician in the 1960's and 1970's and played on over 800 UK charting records, including 54 number 1s.

[7] Peter Sarstedt started his career playing bass in his brother Richard's group –Richard having taken the stage name Eden Kane – before scoring chart success himself in 1969 with the UK number 1 hit "Where Do You Go To My Lovely".

[8] Vicki Haseman was a prolific session singer under her name of Vicki Brown following her marriage to singer/guitarist Joe Brown. She gained great popularity as a solo performer in the Netherlands. Vicki Brown tragically died of breast cancer in June, 1991

[9] Hagstrom produced a range of excellent electric and semi-acoustic guitars and boasted 'the fastest playing neck in the world' I was the owner of a twin cutaway, semi-acoustic Hagstrom 'Viking' model which was a delight to play. Elvis Presley famously borrowed a 1968 Hagstrom Viking II model during the filming of several segments for his 1968 TV special.

[10] Wendy Richard not only made the charts with Mike Sarne, but also gained great acclaim as a TV and film actress, enjoying starring roles in the 1970's sitcom 'Are You Being Served' and over 22 years in the soap opera 'EastEnders'.

Printed in Great Britain
by Amazon